Better Homes and Gardens®

Hometown
FAVORITES

Delicious down-home recipes

Volume 5

Meredith Consumer Marketing
Des Moines, Iowa

Better Homes and Gardens®

Hometown Favorites

MEREDITH CONSUMER MARKETING
Vice President, Consumer Marketing: Janet Donnelly
Consumer Product Marketing Director: Heather Sorensen
Consumer Product Marketing Manager: Wendy Merical
Business Director: Ron Clingman
Senior Production Manager: Al Rodruck

WATERBURY PUBLICATIONS, INC.
Editorial Director: Lisa Kingsley
Associate Editor: Tricia Bergman
Creative Director: Ken Carlson
Associate Design Director: Doug Samuelson
Contributing Art Director: Mindy Samuelson
Contributing Writer: Deborah Wagman
Contributing Copy Editors: Gretchen Kauffman, Peg Smith
Contributing Indexer: Elizabeth T. Parson

BETTER HOMES AND GARDENS® MAGAZINE
Editor in Chief: Gayle Goodson Butler
Deputy Editor, Food and Entertaining: Nancy Wall Hopkins

MEREDITH NATIONAL MEDIA GROUP
President: Tom Harty

MEREDITH CORPORATION
Chairman and Chief Executive Officer: Stephen M. Lacy

In Memoriam: E.T. Meredith III (1933–2003)

Copyright© 2013 by Meredith Corporation.
Des Moines, Iowa.
First Edition. All rights reserved.
Printed in China.
ISSN: 1944-6349 ISBN: 978-0-696-30136-0

Better Homes and Gardens® Test Kitchen

Our seal assures you that every recipe in *Hometown Favorites* has been tested in the Better Homes and Gardens® Test Kitchen. This means that each recipe is practical and reliable, and meets our high standards of taste appeal. We guarantee your satisfaction with this book for as long as you own it.

All of us at Meredith Consumer Marketing are dedicated to providing you with information and ideas to enhance your home. We welcome your comments and suggestions. Write to us at: Meredith Consumer Marketing, 1716 Locust St., Des Moines, IA 50309-3023.

Pictured on front cover:
Salted Almond Brownies, page 171

Contents

CHAPTER 1

Appetizers

Get off to a great start with party-perfect appetizers. From steamy meatballs and dynamite dips to crunchy vegetables and irresistible snack mixes, you'll find hot and cold appetizers for everyone's tastes.

Rich Norwegian Meatballs

Meatballs—especially dark, rich, coffee-spiked ones like these—disappear quickly at parties. Count on three to four meatballs per guest. If you have leftovers, rejoice—these meatballs make a wonderful supper when served over buttered noodles.

PREP: 40 minutes
CHILL: 2 hours
COOK: 24 minutes

72 servings	ingredients	36 servings
1½ cups	soft bread crumbs	¾ cup
½ cup	half-and-half or light cream	¼ cup
¼ cup	strong coffee	2 Tbsp.
2	eggs, lightly beaten	1
¾ cup	finely chopped onion	⅓ cup
¼ cup	finely snipped fresh parsley	2 Tbsp.
1 tsp.	salt	½ tsp.
1 tsp.	freshly grated nutmeg	½ tsp.
¼ tsp.	black pepper	⅛ tsp.
1 lb.	lean ground beef	½ lb.
½ lb.	uncooked ground turkey breast or lean ground pork	¼ lb.
¼ cup	butter	2 Tbsp.
¼ cup	all-purpose flour	2 Tbsp.
1 cup	beef broth	½ cup
1 cup	strong coffee	½ cup
1 tsp.	freshly grated nutmeg	½ tsp.
½ tsp.	salt	¼ tsp.
	Snipped fresh parsley (optional)	

1. In a large bowl combine bread crumbs, half-and-half, and the ¼ cup coffee. Let stand until mixture is evenly moist.

2. Add eggs, onion, parsley, the 1 teaspoon salt, 1 teaspoon nutmeg, and the pepper. Add beef and turkey. Mix well. Cover and chill for 2 hours. With moistened hands, shape mixture into 72 meatballs.

3. In a very large skillet melt 2 tablespoons of the butter over medium heat. Cook half of the meatballs in hot butter about 12 minutes or until done (instant-read thermometer reads 165°F), carefully turning to brown evenly. With a slotted spoon, remove meatballs from skillet. Add remaining butter to skillet and repeat with remaining meatballs. Remove meatballs from skillet.

4. Stir flour into pan drippings until smooth. Add broth, the 1 cup coffee, 1 teaspoon nutmeg, and the ½ teaspoon salt. Cook and stir over medium heat until thickened and bubbly.

5. Return all meatballs to skillet; heat through, gently stirring occasionally. To serve, sprinkle with snipped fresh parsley if desired.

FOR 36 SERVINGS: Prepare using method above, except in Step 1 use 2 tablespoons coffee. In Step 2 use ½ teaspoon salt and ½ teaspoon nutmeg and shape the mixture into 36 meatballs. In Step 3 use 1 tablespoon of the butter. In Step 4 use the ½ cup coffee, ½ teaspoon nutmeg, and the ¼ teaspoon salt.

PER SERVING 30 cal., 2 g total fat (1 g sat. fat), 14 mg chol., 80 mg sodium, 1 g carbo., 0 g fiber, 2 g pro.

Greek Stuffed Meatballs

There's nothing like a slow cooker to help with party preparation. These super-savory lamb meatballs slow-cook to perfection, allowing plenty of time to prepare other dishes you intend to serve.

1. Preheat oven to 350°F. In a large bowl combine egg, bread crumbs, green olives, black olives, parsley, garlic, salt, and pepper. Add beef and lamb; mix until thoroughly combined.

2. Shape some of the meat mixture into a ball around each of 42 cheese cubes, being sure to completely enclose the cheese. Arrange meatballs in a single layer in a 15×10×1-inch baking pan. Bake 25 minutes. Drain well.

3. Place meatballs in a 4- to 5-quart slow cooker. Pour Greek Tomato Sauce over meatballs in cooker; gently toss to coat.

4. Cover and cook on low-heat setting for 3 to 4 hours or on high-heat setting for 1½ to 2 hours. Serve immediately or keep warm, covered, on warm-heat setting or low-heat setting for up to 2 hours.

GREEK TOMATO SAUCE: In a medium saucepan heat 1 tablespoon olive oil over medium heat. Cook ½ cup chopped onion and 1 clove garlic, minced, in hot oil until tender. Stir in 8 ounces canned tomato sauce; ¼ cup dry red wine or beef broth; 1 teaspoon dried oregano, crushed; and ½ teaspoon ground cinnamon. Cook until heated through.

FOR 21 SERVINGS: In Step 2 shape meat mixture around each of 21 cheese cubes. In Step 3 use a 2- to 3½- quart slow cooker.

PER SERVING 104 cal., 7 g total fat (3 g sat. fat), 30 mg chol., 448 mg sodium, 5 g carbo., 1 g fiber, 6 g pro.

PREP: 40 minutes   BAKE: 25 minutes
SLOW COOK: 3 hours (low) or 1½ hours (high)
OVEN: 350°F

42 servings	ingredients	21 servings
2	eggs, lightly beaten	1
1 cup	seasoned fine dry bread crumbs	½ cup
¼ cup	finely chopped pimiento-stuffed green olives	2 Tbsp.
¼ cup	finely chopped black olives	2 Tbsp.
¼ cup	snipped fresh parsley	2 Tbsp.
4 cloves	garlic, minced	2 cloves
1 tsp.	salt	½ tsp.
¼ tsp.	black pepper	⅛ tsp.
1 lb.	lean ground beef	½ lb.
1 lb.	ground lamb	½ lb.
6 oz.	kasseri or feta cheese, cut into ½-inch cubes	3 oz.
1 recipe	Greek Tomato Sauce	½ recipe

Shrimp and Bacon Stuffed Baby Potatoes

Luxury ingredients such as shrimp can be costly to serve at a party—unless you stretch their deliciousness. Here a small, affordable amount of shrimp pairs with everyday bacon and humble potatoes to make an impressive starter.

PREP: 35 minutes
BAKE: 42 minutes
OVEN: 425°F

28 servings	ingredients	14 servings
28	tiny new potatoes	14
¼ cup	Dijon mustard	2 Tbsp.
2 tsp.	olive oil	1 tsp.
2 tsp.	Old Bay seasoning (seafood seasoning)	1 tsp.
2 7- to 8-oz. pkg.	frozen peeled cooked shrimp, thawed, drained, and chopped	1 7- to 8-oz. pkg.
1 8-oz. pkg.	reduced-fat cream cheese (Neufchâtel), softened	½ 8-oz. pkg.
1½ cups	shredded reduced-fat mozzarella cheese	¾ cup
8 slices	bacon, crisp-cooked, drained, and crumbled	4 slices
½ cup	snipped fresh chives (optional)	¼ cup

1. Preheat oven to 425°F. Cut potatoes in half lengthwise. Using a melon baller or a very small spoon, scoop out potato pulp, leaving ¼-inch shells. Cut a thin slice from the bottom of each potato half so it stands upright. Place potatoes, cut sides up, in a 15×10×1-inch baking pan.

2. In a small bowl combine mustard, oil, and 1 teaspoon of the Old Bay seasoning. Brush insides of potato shells with mustard mixture. Bake about 30 minutes or until potatoes are tender.

3. Meanwhile, for filling, in a small bowl combine shrimp, cream cheese, mozzarella cheese, bacon, and the remaining Old Bay seasoning. Spoon filling into potato shells, mounding slightly.

4. Bake for 12 to 15 minutes more or until filling is heated through and cheese melts. Serve warm or at room temperature. If desired, garnish with chives.

FOR 14 SERVINGS: Prepare using method above, except in Step 2 use ½ teaspoon of the Old Bay seasoning.

PER SERVING 96 cal., 4 g total fat (2 g sat. fat), 40 mg chol., 250 mg sodium, 7 g carbo., 1 g fiber, 7 g pro.

Ginger Shrimp Skewers

For the fabulous flavor when making these pretty, bright skewers, opt for freshly grated ginger. Although an entire gingerroot may be more than you need, the reminder may be refrigerated for up to three weeks and frozen for up to six months.

1. Thaw shrimp, if frozen. Peel and devein shrimp, leaving tails intact. In a large saucepan bring the water to boiling. Add shrimp. Simmer, covered, for 1 to 3 minutes or until shrimp are opaque. Drain. Rinse shrimp with cold water; drain.

2. Place shrimp in a resealable plastic bag set in a shallow bowl. Add orange peel, orange juice, vinegar, oil, 2 teaspoons fresh ginger or 1 teaspoon ground ginger, garlic, salt, and cayenne pepper to bag. Seal bag; turn to coat shrimp. Marinate in the refrigerator for 1 to 2 hours.

3. Place pea pods in a steamer basket over boiling water. Cover and steam for 2 to 3 minutes or just until tender. Rinse with cold water; drain.

4. Drain shrimp, discarding marinade. Wrap each shrimp with a pea pod. On each of sixteen 6-inch skewers thread 2 wrapped shrimp and 1 mandarin orange section. If desired, serve with soy sauce.

FOR 8 SERVINGS: Prepare using method above, except in Step 2 use 1 teaspoon fresh ginger or ½ teaspoon ground ginger. In Step 4 use eight 6-inch skewers.

PER SERVING *44 cal., 1 g total fat (0 g sat. fat), 48 mg chol., 58 mg sodium, 2 g carbo., 0 g fiber, 7 g pro.*

MAKE-AHEAD DIRECTIONS: Prepare as directed in Step 1. Place shrimp in an airtight container; seal. Chill for up to 24 hours. Continue as directed.

PREP: 30 minutes
MARINATE: 1 hour

16 servings	ingredients	8 servings
32	fresh or frozen large shrimp in shells	16
3 cups	water	1½ cups
2 tsp.	finely shredded orange peel	1 tsp.
6 Tbsp.	orange juice	3 Tbsp.
2 Tbsp.	white wine vinegar	1 Tbsp.
2 tsp.	toasted sesame oil or olive oil	1 tsp.
2 tsp. or 1 tsp.	grated fresh ginger or ground ginger	1 tsp. or ½ tsp.
2 cloves	garlic, minced	1 clove
¼ tsp.	salt	⅛ tsp.
¼ tsp.	cayenne pepper	⅛ tsp.
32	fresh pea pods	16
16	canned mandarin orange sections	8
	Reduced-sodium soy sauce (optional)	

Olive-Cherry Bruschetta

Here's an ingredient list that may have you raising your eyebrows. Two kinds of olives, dried cherries, hot cherry peppers, lime basil, and goat cheese? Trust us—each of these seemingly incongruous ingredients makes a palate-pleasing complement to its pals.

PREP: 45 minutes
BAKE: 5 minutes
OVEN: 425°F

32 servings	ingredients	16 servings
32	¾-inch-thick slices rustic baguette-style sourdough bread	16
6 Tbsp.	olive oil	3 Tbsp.
	Salt and black pepper	
1 cup	pimiento-stuffed Spanish Manzanilla olives, sliced	½ cup
½ cup	Kalamata pitted olives, chopped	¼ cup
½ cup	dried tart cherries, snipped	¼ cup
¼ cup	bottled whole hot cherry peppers, seeded and chopped	2 Tbsp.
1 large	shallot, quartered and thinly sliced	1 small
1 Tbsp.	snipped fresh basil	1½ tsp.
1 tsp.	finely shredded lime peel	½ tsp.
2 tsp.	fresh lime juice	1 tsp.
2 oz.	thinly sliced prosciutto	1 oz.
6 oz.	goat cheese (chèvre)	3 oz.

1. Position oven rack in center of oven. Preheat oven to 425°F. Place baguette slices on a very large baking sheet. Brush slices with 4 tablespoons of the oil, then season lightly with salt and black pepper. Toast bread about 5 minutes until crisp and lightly browned, turning once. Remove from oven; set aside.

2. For olive-cherry tapenade, in a medium bowl stir together the remaining 2 tablespoons oil, olives, cherries, peppers, shallot, basil, lime peel, and lime juice.

3. Cut prosciutto into 32 pieces. Spread goat cheese on toast slices. Top with prosciutto and olive-cherry tapenade.

FOR 16 SERVINGS: Prepare using method above, except in Step 1 brush slices with 2 tablespoons of the oil. In Step 2 use the remaining 1 tablespoon oil. In Step 3 cut prosciutto into 16 pieces.

PER SERVING 104 *cal.,* 5 *g total fat (*2 *g sat. fat),* 4 *mg chol.,* 294 *mg sodium,* 11 *g carbo.,* 1 *g fiber,* 3 *g pro.*

Salami Crostini

This spicy mixture resembles French pâté, but that's where the similarity ends. When spread or dabbed on crispy baguette slices, the flavor of this quick and easy mixture is 100 percent Italian.

1. Prepare Crostini. Cut salami into large chunks. Place in a food processor; cover and process until finely chopped. Add cheese, mustard, and chives; cover and process until nearly smooth.

2. Transfer salami mixture to a small serving bowl. If necessary, stir in enough milk to reach spreading consistency. Serve with crostini.

CROSTINI: Preheat oven to 400°F. Cut two 8-ounce loaves baguette-style French bread into ½-inch diagonal slices. Arrange bread slices on a large baking sheet. Lightly brush one side of bread slices with olive oil. Bake about 8 minutes or until lightly browned, turning once. Cool.

FOR 24 SERVINGS: Prepare using method above, except when making the Crostini use one 8-ounce loaf baguette-style French bread.

PER SERVING 61 cal., 3 g total fat (1 g sat. fat), 6 mg chol., 163 mg sodium, 5 g carbo., 0 g fiber, 2 g pro.

PREP: 20 minutes
BAKE: 8 minutes
OVEN: 400°F

48 servings	ingredients	24 servings
	Crostini	
8 oz.	soft Italian salami (such as Genoa or Toscano)	4 oz.
½ cup	ricotta cheese	¼ cup
8 tsp.	spicy brown mustard or smoky mustard	4 tsp.
2 Tbsp.	coarsely snipped fresh chives	1 Tbsp.
	Milk (optional)	

Pecan, Cherry, and Brie Bites

What a fun take on the traditional pastry-wrapped Brie cheese. Toasty baked squares of puff pastry are filled with soft and gooey cherries, toasted pecans, and soft cheese.

1. Preheat oven to 375°F. Line a large baking sheet with parchment paper; set aside. Unfold puff pastry on a lightly floured surface. Using a sharp knife or a pastry wheel, cut pastry into 1½-inch squares. Place pastry squares 1 inch apart on the prepared baking sheet.

2. In a small bowl combine egg and the water. Lightly brush egg mixture onto pastry squares. In another small bowl combine salt, thyme, and pepper. Sprinkle mixture over pastry squares.

3. Bake for 10 to 12 minutes or until pastry is puffed and golden brown. Cool slightly.

4. Meanwhile, in a small bowl combine pecans, dried cherries, and honey. Cut Brie into small wedges. Place a wedge of Brie on a piece of pastry; top with some of the pecan mixture. Place another piece of pastry on top. If desired, sprinkle with snipped fresh thyme.

PER SERVING *359 cal., 25 g total fat (9 g sat. fat), 55 mg chol., 364 mg sodium, 25 g carbo., 2 g fiber, 10 g pro.*

HAZELNUT- AND-APRICOT-TOPPED BRIE: Prepare as directed, except substitute chopped hazelnuts (filberts) or almonds for the pecans, snipped dried apricots for the dried cherries, and apricot preserves for the honey.

PREP: 25 minutes
BAKE: 10 minutes
OVEN: 375°F

16 servings	ingredients	8 servings
1 17.3 oz. pkg.	frozen puff pastry sheets, thawed	½ 17.3-oz. pkg.
2	eggs, lightly beaten	1
2 Tbsp.	water	1 Tbsp.
1 tsp.	coarse salt	½ tsp.
1 tsp.	snipped fresh thyme	½ tsp.
½ tsp.	freshly ground black pepper	¼ tsp.
1 cup	chopped pecans, toasted (see note, page 102)	½ cup
⅔ cup	snipped dried tart cherries	⅓ cup
4 Tbsp.	honey	2 Tbsp.
2 8-oz. rounds	Brie cheese	1 8-oz. round
	snipped fresh thyme (optional)	

Herbed Dijon-Marinated Veggies

Vegetables do not benefit from excessive marinating, so to keep the veggies bright and beautiful, stick to the recipe's suggested time frame. To add more texture to the mixture, choose whole-grain Dijon mustard.

1. In a large bowl whisk together wine, basil, parsley, oil, 4 teaspoons fresh thyme or oregano (or 1 teaspoon dried thyme or oregano, crushed), mustard, garlic, and salt. Add mushrooms, tomatoes, sweet pepper, and zucchini; toss gently to coat.

2. Cover vegetables and marinate at room temperature for 30 to 60 minutes, stirring occasionally. Using a slotted spoon, transfer vegetables to a serving bowl.

FOR 6 SERVINGS: Prepare using method above, except in Step 1 use 2 teaspoons fresh thyme or oregano (or ½ teaspoon dried thyme or oregano, crushed).

PER SERVING 52 cal., 3 g total fat (0 g sat. fat), 0 mg chol., 143 mg sodium, 5 g carbo., 1 g fiber, 2 g pro.

PREP: 20 minutes
MARINATE: 30 minutes

12 servings	ingredients	6 servings
6 Tbsp.	dry white wine (such as Pinot Grigio or Sauvignon Blanc)	3 Tbsp.
4 Tbsp.	snipped fresh basil	2 Tbsp.
2 Tbsp.	snipped fresh parsley	1 Tbsp.
2 Tbsp.	olive oil	1 Tbsp.
4 tsp.	snipped fresh thyme or oregano	2 tsp.
4 tsp.	Dijon mustard	2 tsp.
2 cloves	garlic, minced	1 clove
½ tsp.	salt	¼ tsp.
3 cups	fresh small cremini mushrooms	1½ cups
2 cups	grape or cherry tomatoes	1 cup
2 cups	yellow and/or orange sweet pepper strips	1 cup
2 (2 cups)	zucchini, quartered lengthwise and cut into 1-inch pieces	1 (1 cup)

Mini Gruyère Puffs

Although these little clouds of cheesy goodness are fabulous straight from the oven and enjoyed as is, they may also be sliced horizontally and used to make adorable capped containers for tapenade and tuna, ham and egg salad.

1. Preheat oven to 450°F. Grease a baking sheet; set aside. In a small saucepan combine the water, butter, basil, garlic salt, and cayenne pepper. Bring to boiling over medium heat, stirring to melt butter. Immediately add flour all at once, stirring vigorously. Cook and stir until mixture forms a ball that doesn't separate. Remove from heat. Cool for 5 minutes.

2. Add eggs, one at a time, to mixture in saucepan, beating with a spoon after each addition until smooth. Stir in shredded Gruyère cheese. Drop dough by rounded teaspoons about 2 inches apart onto the prepared baking sheet.* Sprinkle with Parmesan cheese.

3. Bake for 10 minutes. Reduce oven temperature to 375°F. Bake for 10 to 12 minutes more or until puffed and golden. Turn off oven. Let puffs stand in oven for 3 minutes. Sprinkle lightly with grated Gruyère cheese. Transfer puffs to a wire rack; cool completely.

*NOTE: If you prefer to pipe the dough, fit a pastry bag with a ½-inch open star tip. Spoon dough into bag. Pipe small mounds of dough about 2 inches apart onto the prepared baking sheet.

PER SERVING 53 cal., 4 g total fat (2 g sat. fat), 31 mg chol., 76 mg sodium, 2 g carbo., 0 g fiber, 2 g pro.

PREP: 15 minutes   COOL: 5 minutes
BAKE: 20 minutes   STAND: 3 minutes
OVEN: 450°F/375°F

40 servings	ingredients	20 servings
1 cup	water	½ cup
½ cup	butter	¼ cup
1 tsp.	dried basil, crushed	½ tsp.
½ tsp.	garlic salt	¼ tsp.
⅛ tsp.	cayenne pepper	Dash
1 cup	all-purpose flour	½ cup
4	eggs	2
1 cup	shredded Gruyère cheese or Swiss cheese	½ cup
4 Tbsp.	grated Parmesan cheese	2 Tbsp.
	Grated Gruyère cheese or Swiss cheese	

Marinated Feta

If make-ahead appetizers fit your lifestyle, look no further. Marinated cubes of feta have the sort of rustic, natural beauty that adds a touch of casual sophistication to your table—and they may be prepared up to five days ahead!

1. In a small bowl combine olive oil, herbs, lemon juice, garlic, and cracked peppercorns. Stir until well mixed. Add cheese cubes; toss very gently to coat. Divide between two clean half-pint jars with tight-fitting lids.

2. Seal jars; chill for at least 3 days or up to 5 days.

3. Let stand at room temperature for 30 minutes before serving.

PER SERVING 107 cal., 9 g total fat (5 g sat. fat), 25 mg chol., 317 mg sodium, 2 g carbo., 0 g fiber, 4 g pro.

PREP: 15 minutes
CHILL: 3 days
STAND: 30 minutes

16 servings	ingredients	8 servings
4 Tbsp.	olive oil	2 Tbsp.
4 Tbsp.	snipped assorted fresh herbs, such as oregano, basil, thyme, and/or parsley	2 Tbsp.
2 Tbsp.	lemon juice	1 Tbsp.
4 cloves	garlic, minced	2 cloves
1 tsp.	peppercorn melange, cracked	½ tsp.
16 oz.	feta cheese, cubed	8 oz.

Gorgonzola-Thyme Stuffed Olives

Gorgonzola is the Italian version of blue cheese. Like its French, English, and American counterparts, it packs a punch—so a little goes a long way. If you are unable to find pimiento-free green olives, push the pimientoes through the hole with a drinking straw, then save them to use in a creamy casserole.

1. In a medium bowl beat Gorgonzola cheese and cream cheese with an electric mixer on medium until creamy. Stir in thyme and pepper.

2. Spoon cheese mixture into a pastry bag fitted with a small plain round tip. Pipe cheese filling into each olive.

PER SERVING *19 cal., 2 g total fat (1 g sat. fat), 3 mg chol., 100 mg sodium, 0 g carbo., 0 g fiber, 1 g pro.*

START TO FINISH: **25 minutes**

40 servings	ingredients	20 servings
3 oz.	gorgonzola cheese, crumbled	1½ oz.
2 oz.	cream cheese, softened	1 oz.
2 tsp.	snipped fresh thyme	1 tsp.
½ tsp.	black pepper	¼ tsp.
40	whole pitted green olives	20

Sweet and Spicy Nuts

Unlike more complicated spiced nut recipes that require making sugar syrup or butter mixtures to adhere seasonings to the nuts, this one relies on a humble egg white! For superlative flavor, make sure all your spices are fresh.

1. Preheat oven to 300°F. In a medium bowl beat egg white and water until frothy. Add nuts and toss to coat. Transfer to a wire mesh sieve; drain nuts for 5 minutes.

2. Meanwhile, in a large plastic bag combine the sugar, salt, cumin, paprika, coriander, cayenne pepper, and ginger. Add the nuts; shake well to coat with the spice mixture. Spread nuts evenly in an ungreased 15×10×1-inch baking pan.

3. Bake for 35 to 40 minutes until nuts are toasted and spice mixture is dry, stirring every 10 minutes. Remove from oven; transfer to a sheet of foil. Cool completely. Break nuts apart.

PER SERVING *242 cal., 18 g total fat (3 g sat. fat), 0 mg chol., 399 mg sodium, 18 g carbo., 1 g fiber, 6 g pro.*

PREP: 10 minutes
BAKE: 35 minutes
OVEN: 300°F

24 servings	ingredients	12 servings
2	egg whites	1
2 Tbsp.	water	1 Tbsp.
2 lb.	raw whole cashews, whole almonds, walnut halves, and/or pecan halves	1 lb.
⅔ cup	sugar	⅓ cup
4 tsp.	salt	2 tsp
3 tsp.	ground cumin	1½ tsp.
2 tsp.	paprika	1 tsp.
2 tsp.	ground coriander	1 tsp.
1 tsp.	cayenne pepper	½ tsp.
½ tsp.	ground ginger	¼ tsp.

Tomato and Basil Chèvre Spread

If you are lucky enough to have any of this sensational spread left over after the party, tuck it into tomorrow morning's omelet along with a bit of finely diced ham and enjoy it all over again.

1. In a small bowl cover dried tomatoes with boiling water; let stand for 10 minutes. Drain tomatoes, discarding liquid. Finely snip tomatoes.

2. In a medium bowl stir together snipped tomatoes, goat cheese, cream cheese, basil, garlic, and pepper. Stir in enough of the milk to make mixture spreading consistency. Cover and chill for 2 to 4 hours. Serve with miniature toasts and/or crackers.

PER SERVING 66 cal., 5 g total fat (3 g sat. fat), 14 mg chol., 125 mg sodium, 2 g carbo., 0 g fiber, 4 g pro.

PREP: 15 minutes
STAND: 10 minutes
CHILL: 2 hours

24 servings	ingredients	12 servings
⅔ cup	dried tomatoes (not oil-packed)	⅓ cup
8 oz.	soft goat cheese (chèvre)	4 oz.
1 8-oz. pkg.	reduced-fat cream cheese (Neufchâtel), softened	½ 8-oz. pkg.
½ cup or 2 tsp.	snipped fresh basil or dried basil, crushed	¼ cup or 1 tsp.
6 cloves	garlic, minced	3 cloves
¼ tsp.	black pepper	⅛ tsp.
2 to 4 Tbsp.	fat-free milk	1 to 2 Tbsp.
	Miniature toasts and/or assorted reduced-fat crackers	

Pumpkin Pesto

Goodbye, pie. Hello appetizer! Pumpkin is delicious when paired with savory ingredients. Look carefully when purchasing canned pumpkin, to make sure that you select pure pumpkin rather than pumpkin pie filling.

1. In a food processor combine basil, parsley, pumpkin, walnuts, the ½ cup cheese, honey, garlic, lemon juice, salt, and pepper. Cover and process with several on/off pulses until mixture is coarsely chopped. With food processor running, add oil in a thin, steady stream. (When necessary, stop processor and scrape down side of bowl.)

2. Transfer pesto to a serving bowl. If desired, garnish with additional cheese. Serve with toasted pita wedges, baguette slices, and/or crackers.

FOR 14 SERVINGS: Prepare using method above, except in Step 1 use the ¼ cup cheese.

PER SERVING 60 cal., 4 g total fat (1 g sat. fat), 1 mg chol., 70 mg sodium, 5 g carbo., 1 g fiber, 1 g pro.

START TO FINISH: 15 minutes

28 servings	ingredients	14 servings
2 cups	packed fresh basil leaves	1 cup
2 cups	packed fresh parsley leaves	1 cup
2 cups	canned pumpkin	1 cup
⅔ cup	chopped toasted walnuts (see note, page 102)	⅓ cup
½ cup	finely shredded Parmesan cheese	¼ cup
4 Tbsp.	honey	2 Tbsp.
6 cloves	garlic, minced	3 cloves
2 tsp.	lemon juice	1 tsp.
½ tsp.	salt	¼ tsp.
½ tsp.	black pepper	¼ tsp.
4 Tbsp.	olive oil	2 Tbsp.
	Finely shredded Parmesan cheese (optional)	
	Toasted pita wedges, baguette slices, and/or assorted crackers	

Miniature Bread Bowls with Dip

PREP: 20 minutes
BAKE: 8 minutes
OVEN: 400°F

24 servings	ingredients	12 servings
24	unsliced cocktail-size buns	12
½ cup	butter, melted	¼ cup
2 Tbsp.	purchased garlic puree	1 Tbsp.
2 15-oz. jars	creamy spinach dip	1 15-oz. jar
	Assorted fresh vegetables such as carrots, snow peas, and red sweet peppers	

These cuter-than-cute appetizers can be made in a moment's notice, making them perfect for impromptu gatherings and after-work get-togethers.

1. Preheat oven to 400°F. Using a serrated knife, hollow out each bun by cutting around the top at an angle toward the center. Remove bread centers and, if desired, reserve for another use.

2. In a small bowl combine melted butter and garlic. Generously brush insides and outsides of bowls with butter mixture. Arrange bowls 2 inches apart on a large baking sheet.

3. Bake for 8 to 10 minutes or until lightly browned.

4. If desired, heat spinach dip. To serve, spoon about 2 tablespoons dip into each warm bread bowl. (If using soup, heat through and spoon into bread bowls just before serving.) Serve with assorted vegetables.

MAKE-AHEAD DIRECTIONS: Prepare and bake bread bowls as directed. Transfer to a storage container and store at room temperature for up to 24 hours. To serve, preheat oven to 350°F. Arrange bread bowls on a baking sheet and bake for 3 to 5 minutes until warm. Fill as directed.

PER SERVING *178 cal., 10 g total fat (3 g sat. fat), 14 mg chol., 408 mg sodium, 17 g carbo., 1 g fiber, 4 g pro.*

Roasted Corn and Crab Dip

All it take is a quick 20 minutes in the oven to infuse frozen corn kernels with the taste of fresh, grill-caramelized corn on the cob, making it a superlative accompaniment to sweet, rich crabmeat in this dreamy dip.

PREP: 25 minutes **ROAST:** 20 minutes
BAKE: 20 minutes **OVEN:** 425°F/375°F

20 servings	ingredients	10 servings
	Nonstick cooking spray	
2 cups	frozen whole kernel corn, thawed	1 cup
2 cups	chopped red sweet pepper	1 cup
4 tsp.	olive oil	2 tsp.
2 cups or 1 6-oz. can	cooked crabmeat or crabmeat, drained, flaked, and cartilage removed	1 cup ½ 6-oz. can
2 cups	shredded Monterey Jack cheese with jalapeño chile peppers	1 cup
⅔ cup	mayonnaise	⅓ cup
½ cup	sour cream	¼ cup
½ cup	sliced green onions	¼ cup
½ tsp.	freshly ground black pepper	¼ tsp.
	Broken tostada shells, toasted baguette-style French bread slices, and/or crackers	

1. Preheat oven to 425°F. Lightly coat a 2-quart shallow baking dish with cooking spray; set aside. In a shallow baking pan combine corn and sweet pepper. Drizzle with olive oil; toss to coat. Roast, uncovered, about 20 minutes or until vegetables start to brown, stirring occasionally. Remove from oven and cool. Reduce oven temperature to 375°F.

2. Meanwhile, in a medium bowl stir together crabmeat, cheese, mayonnaise, sour cream, green onions, and black pepper. Stir in roasted vegetables. Transfer mixture to prepared dish.

3. Bake about 20 minutes or until bubbly around edges. Serve with toasted broken tostada shells.

FOR 10 SERVINGS: Prepare using method above, except in Step 1 use a 1-quart shallow baking dish.

PER SERVING 151 cal., 12 g total fat (4 g sat. fat), 29 mg chol., 180 mg sodium, 5 g carbo., 1 g fiber, 7 g pro.

Creamy Fennel and Leek Dip

Leeks tend to capture sand and debris between layers. Slice it lengthwise and wash well before slicing. And be sure to reserve the graceful, frilly fennel fronds for garnish.

1. Preheat oven to 350°F. In a large skillet cook pancetta in olive oil over medium heat until golden brown. Add fennel and leeks; cook about 10 minutes or until tender and just starting to brown, stirring occasionally. Remove from heat; let cool.

2. In a medium bowl combine mayonnaise, sour cream, 1½ cups of the Asiago cheese, the whipping cream, salt, and crushed red pepper.* Stir in the cooled fennel mixture. Transfer to a 2-quart shallow baking dish or individual-size baking dishes. Sprinkle with the remaining ½ cup Asiago cheese.

3. Bake about 20 minutes or until bubbly around edges. Serve with toasted baguette slices.

FOR 12 SERVINGS: Prepare using method above, except in Step 2 use ¾ cup of the Asiago cheese and a 1-quart shallow baking dish or individual-size baking dishes. Sprinkle with remaining ¼ cup cheese.

*NOTE If desired, reserve ½ cup mixture for topping. Unless serving immediately, place reserved, mixture in an airtight container; chill for up to 24 hours. After baking, top with reserved fennel and leek mixture and bake for additional 5 minutes.

PER SERVING 188 cal., 17 g total fat (6 g sat. fat), 29 mg chol., 370 mg sodium, 6 g carbo., 1 g fiber, 4 g pro.

PREP: 20 minutes   COOK: 12 minutes
BAKE: 20 minutes   OVEN: 350°F

24 servings	ingredients	12 servings
4 oz.	pancetta, finely chopped	2 oz.
2 Tbsp.	olive oil	1 Tbsp.
4 bulbs	fennel, halved lengthwise, cored, and thinly sliced	2 bulbs
4	leeks, thinly sliced	2
1 cup	mayonnaise or salad dressing	½ cup
1 cup	sour cream	½ cup
2 cups	grated Asiago cheese or Parmesan cheese	1 cup
½ cup	whipping cream	¼ cup
1 tsp.	salt	½ tsp.
1 tsp.	crushed red pepper	½ tsp.
	Baguette-style French bread, sliced and toasted	

Eggplant Dip

The key to making this dip is to start with excellent eggplants. Select those with smooth, glossy, dark purple skin that feel heavy for their size. Eggplants become bitter with age, so use them within a day or two of purchase.

PREP: 45 minutes
ROAST: 40 minutes
OVEN: 400°F

40 servings	ingredients	20 servings
4 lb.	eggplants or baby eggplants	2 lb.
4 bulbs	garlic	2 bulbs
1 cup	olive oil	½ cup
4 tsp.	salt	2 tsp.
3 cups	coarsely chopped red sweet peppers	1½ cups
⅔ cup	lemon juice	⅓ cup
½ cup	snipped fresh parsley	¼ cup
¼ cup	snipped fresh oregano	2 Tbsp.
	Fresh oregano leaves (optional)	
	Toasted baguette-style French bread, sliced, or flatbread, broken into pieces	

1. Preheat oven to 400°F. Wash eggplants; trim and cut into ½- to 1-inch pieces. Divide eggplant between two 15×10×1-inch baking pans or shallow roasting pans. Using a sharp knife, cut off the top ½ inch from garlic bulbs to expose individual cloves. Leaving garlic bulbs whole, remove any loose, papery outer layers. Place garlic bulbs on a 12-inch square of heavy foil; drizzle with 1 tablespoon of the olive oil. Wrap foil up around the garlic bulbs to completely enclose.

2. Drizzle ¼ cup of the remaining olive oil over eggplant in each pan and sprinkle half of the salt over eggplant in each pan; toss to coat. Place eggplant and garlic packet in oven, placing pans on separate oven racks. Roast for 20 minutes, stirring eggplant once. Add half of the sweet peppers to each pan with eggplant; stir to combine. Roast about 20 minutes more or until vegetables are tender, stirring once. Remove pans and garlic from oven and cool.

3. Transfer eggplant and peppers to a very large glass or nonreactive bowl. Squeeze garlic pulp from individual cloves into a small bowl; using the back of a spoon, mash garlic pulp. Add the remaining olive oil and the lemon juice to garlic; whisk to combine. Add garlic mixture, parsley, and snipped oregano to eggplant mixture; toss to combine.

4. If desired, garnish with oregano leaves. Serve with flatbread.

FOR 20 SERVINGS: Prepare using method above, except in Step 1 use one baking pan and 1½ teaspoons of the olive oil. In Step 2 drizzle 2 tablespoons of the remaining olive oil.

PER SERVING *67 cal., 6 g total fat (1 g sat. fat), 0 mg chol., 235 mg sodium, 4 g carbo., 2 g fiber, 1 g pro.*

Sweet Yogurt Fruit Dip

Health-minded guests always appreciate finding a healthful option on the buffet table, and this dip—which begins with high-protein, low-fat Greek yogurt—is bound to please.

1. In a small bowl combine yogurt, maple syrup, the ½ teaspoon cinnamon, nutmeg, and cloves. If desired, sprinkle dip with additional ground cinnamon. Serve fruit with dip.

FOR 6 SERVINGS: Prepare using method above, except in Step 1 use ¼ teaspoon cinnamon.

PER SERVING *67 cal., 1 g total fat (0 g sat. fat), 1 mg chol., 10 mg sodium, 14 g carbo., 2 g fiber, 3 g pro.*

START TO FINISH: **15 minutes**

12 servings	ingredients	6 servings
2 6-oz. cartons	plain low-fat Greek yogurt	1 6-oz. carton
2 Tbsp.	maple syrup	1 Tbsp.
½ tsp.	ground cinnamon	¼ tsp.
¼ tsp.	ground nutmeg	⅛ tsp.
⅛ tsp.	ground cloves	Dash
	Ground cinnamon (optional)	
2	apples, cored and cut into wedges	1
2	pears, cored and cut into wedges	1
2 cups	strawberries	1 cup

Confetti Peanut Butter Munchies

A big bowl of this crisp and crunchy mixture will not only be the life of the party, but kids will love finding a small bag in their lunches. And it also makes a high-energy trail mix for camping and hiking.

1. In an extra-large bowl or roaster combine cereal and pretzels; set aside. In a small saucepan combine chocolate pieces, peanut butter, and butter. Stir over medium-low heat until melted. Remove from heat. Stir in vanilla. Pour chocolate mixture over cereal mixture; toss gently to coat.

2. Place powdered sugar in a large resealable plastic bag. Add cereal mixture; seal bag and shake to coat. Spread cereal mixture on a sheet of waxed paper and let stand about 1 hour or until set.

3. In an extra-large bowl combine cereal mixture, mango, pineapple, cranberries, and raisins.

PER SERVING *212 cal., 8 g total fat (3 g sat. fat), 6 mg chol., 199 mg sodium, 36 g carbo., 1 g fiber, 3 g pro.*

PREP: 25 minutes
STAND: 1 hour

44 servings	ingredients	22 servings
14 cups	crispy corn and rice cereal	7 cups
4 cups	pretzel sticks or nuggets	2 cups
2 cups	semisweet chocolate pieces	1 cup
1 cup	peanut butter	½ cup
½ cup	butter	¼ cup
2 tsp.	vanilla	1 tsp.
4 cups	powdered sugar	2 cups
1 cup	dried mango, coarsely chopped	½ cup
1 cup	dried pineapple, coarsely chopped	½ cup
½ cup	dried cranberries	¼ cup
½ cup	golden raisins	¼ cup

CHAPTER 2

Poultry

Chicken and turkey—our fine-feathered friends—possess a quality that allows them to work well with an enormous variety of seasonings, flavors and cooking techniques—and you'll find some sensational selections here.

36

61

68

Cinnamon-Roasted Chicken with Pumpkin-Sage Grits

This unusual combination of ingredients creates a comforting, Southern-style supper in a matter of minutes. Spooning the pumpkin grits onto warmed plates will help retain their warm, creamy goodness.

1. Preheat oven to 400°F. Arrange chicken breast halves in two 13×9×2-inch baking pans. Drizzle chicken with oil and sprinkle with 2 teaspoons of the salt, the cinnamon, and black pepper. Rub the spices over all sides of the chicken. Roast in preheated oven 18 to 20 minutes or until no longer pink and juices run clear.

2. Meanwhile, in a large saucepan bring water to boiling. Stir in grits until combined. Stir in pumpkin, sage, and 1 teaspoon salt. Return to boiling; reduce heat. Cook, uncovered, for 5 to 7 minutes or until thickened, stirring frequently. Remove from heat; stir in cheese.

3. To serve, spoon grits onto dinner plates and top with chicken breast halves.

FOR 4 SERVINGS: Prepare using method above, except in Step 1 use one 13×9×2-inch baking pan and 1 teaspoon of the salt. In Step 2 use a medium saucepan and ½ teaspoon salt.

PER SERVING 253 cal., 8 g total fat (3 g sat. fat), 76 mg chol., 1,162 mg sodium, 14 g carbo., 2 g fiber, 30 g pro.

PREP: 10 minutes
ROAST: 18 minutes
OVEN: 400°F

8 servings	ingredients	4 servings
8	4-oz. skinless, boneless chicken breast halves	4
2 Tbsp.	vegetable oil	1 Tbsp.
3 tsp.	salt	1½ tsp.
2 tsp.	ground cinnamon	1 tsp.
1 tsp.	black pepper	½ tsp.
3 cups	water	1½ cups
1⅓ cups	instant grits	⅔ cup
1 cup	canned pumpkin	½ cup
2 Tbsp.	snipped fresh sage	1 Tbsp.
⅔ cup	shredded cheddar cheese	⅓ cup

Citrus-Herb Marinated Chicken

PREP: 20 minutes
MARINATE: 2 hours
BROIL: 12 minutes

8 servings	ingredients	4 servings
8	4-oz. skinless, boneless chicken breast halves	4
⅔ cup	lemon juice or orange juice	⅓ cup
2 Tbsp.	honey	1 Tbsp.
2 Tbsp.	olive oil	1 Tbsp.
2 Tbsp.	snipped fresh thyme	1 Tbsp.
4 tsp.	snipped fresh rosemary	2 tsp.
4 Tbsp.	finely chopped shallot	2 Tbsp.
2 cloves	garlic, minced	1 clove
1 tsp.	salt	½ tsp.
½ tsp.	freshly ground black pepper	¼ tsp.
	Lemon or orange wedges (optional)	

The sunny-fresh flavors of these marinated chicken breasts call for the simplest of accompaniments. If you make this dish in spring, roasted asparagus would be perfect. In the fall, consider broccoli steamed just until crisp-tender.

1. Place chicken breast halves in a resealable plastic bag set in a shallow dish. For marinade, stir together lemon juice; honey; olive oil; fresh thyme (or 2 teaspoons dried thyme, crushed); fresh rosemary (or 1 teaspoon dried rosemary crushed); shallot; garlic; salt; and pepper. Pour over chicken; seal the bag. Marinate in the refrigerator for 2 to 4 hours, turning the bag occasionally.

2. Preheat broiler. Drain chicken, reserving marinade. Place chicken on the unheated rack of a broiler pan. Broil 4 to 5 inches from the heat about 6 minutes or until lightly browned.

3. Turn chicken and brush lightly with reserved marinade. Discard any remaining marinade. Broil for 6 to 8 minutes more or until chicken is no longer pink (170°F). If desired, serve with lemon wedges.

FOR 4 SERVINGS: Prepare using method above, except in Step 1 use fresh thyme or 1 teaspoon dried thyme, crushed, and fresh rosemary or ½ teaspoon dried rosemary, crushed.

PER SERVING *212 cal., 5 g total fat (1 g sat. fat), 82 mg chol., 366 mg sodium, 7 g carbo., 0 g fiber, 33 g pro.*

Greek Braised Chicken Legs

Chicken legs are often an overlooked cut, and that is a shame because—when slow-cooked—drumsticks are the richest, most moist, and flavorful part of the bird. Give these Greek-style drumsticks a go and see for yourself.

1. Place onion slices in a 5- to 6-quart slow cooker. Sprinkle drumsticks with Greek seasoning. Place drumsticks on top of onion in cooker. Top drumsticks with tomatoes, olives, and garlic.

2. Cover and cook on low-heat setting for 6 to 8 hours or on high-heat setting for 3 to 4 hours.

3. Using a slotted spoon, serve chicken mixture over hot cooked brown rice. If desired, spoon some of the cooking liquid over top. Sprinkle with parsley and lemon peel.

FOR 4 SERVINGS: Prepare using method above, except in Step 1 use a 3½- or 4-quart slow cooker.

PER SERVING 404 cal., 9 g total fat (2 g sat. fat), 157 mg chol., 338 mg sodium, 32 g carbo., 4 g fiber, 46 g pro.

PREP: 25 minutes
SLOW COOK: 6 hours (low) or 3 hours (high)

8 servings	ingredients	4 servings
2	medium onions, sliced	1
16	chicken drumsticks skinned	8
2 tsp.	Greek seasoning	1 tsp.
6 cups	halved grape tomatoes or cherry tomatoes	3 cups
½ cup	chopped pimiento-stuffed green olives	¼ cup
8 cloves	garlic, minced	4 cloves
4 cups	hot cooked brown rice	2 cups
½ cup	snipped fresh parsley or parsley sprigs	¼ cup
2 tsp.	finely shredded lemon peel	1 tsp.

Oven-Fried Chicken with Tomato Gravy

A dip in Greek yogurt imbues these crunchy, coated chicken breasts with a buttermilklike tanginess. And the ridiculously simple, three-ingredient tomato gravy plays along, providing a light but tangy accompaniment.

1. Preheat oven to 425°F. Lightly coat a baking sheet with cooking spray. Set aside.

2. In a shallow dish combine yogurt and honey. In another shallow dish combine corn flakes and ½ cup of the basil. Cut chicken crosswise into 16 pieces. Arrange chicken pieces on a tray; cover with plastic wrap. Pound lightly with the flat side of a meat mallet to make of uniform thickness. Season chicken with salt and pepper. Dip chicken in yogurt mixture in shallow dish to coat and then in corn flake mixture. Place on prepared baking sheet. Bake for 15 to 18 minutes or until chicken is crisp and golden on outside and no pink remains on inside (170°F).

3. Meanwhile, in a small saucepan combine undrained tomatoes, Worcestershire, and remaining ½ cup basil. Cook and stir over medium-low heat until heated through.

4. Serve tomato sauce alongside chicken.

FOR 4 SERVINGS: Prepare using method above, except in Step 2 use ¼ cup of the basil and in Step 3 use the remaining ¼ cup basil. Cut chicken crosswise into 8 pieces.

PER SERVING *301 cal., 6 g total fat (3 g sat. fat), 80 mg chol., 634 mg sodium, 32 g carbo., 3 g fiber, 30 g pro.*

PREP: **15 minutes**
BAKE: **15 minutes**
OVEN: **425°F**

8 servings	ingredients	4 servings
	Nonstick cooking spray	
2 6-oz. containers	plain Greek yogurt	1 6-oz. container
4 Tbsp.	honey	2 Tbsp.
5 cups	corn flakes, coarsely crushed	2½ cups
1 cup	basil leaves, snipped	½ cup
8	skinless, boneless chicken breast halves	4
	Salt and black pepper	
2 14.5-oz. cans	fire-roasted tomatoes with garlic	1 14.5-oz. can
4 tsp.	Worcestershire sauce	2 tsp.

Chicken and Fettuccine with Artichokes

8 servings	ingredients	4 servings
8 oz.	dried fettuccine or linguine	4 oz.
2 Tbsp.	olive oil	1 Tbsp.
12 oz.	skinless, boneless chicken breast halves	6 oz.
¼ cup	butter	2 Tbsp.
3 cloves	garlic, minced	1 clove
1 8-oz. pkg.	frozen halved and quartered artichoke hearts, thawed	½ 8-oz. pkg.
¾ cup	dry white wine	⅓ cup
¼ cup	coarsely chopped pistachio nuts	2 Tbsp.
¼ tsp.	salt	⅛ tsp.
2 Tbsp.	snipped fresh parsley	1 Tbsp.
	Chopped pistachio nuts (optional)	
	Cracked black pepper (optional)	
	Grated Parmesan cheese (optional)	

Concocted with ingredients commonly found in the pantry, fridge, and freezer, this ready-in-30-minutes recipe brings upscale Italian cuisine to the table with no trouble at all.

1. Cook pasta according to package directions; drain. Return pasta to hot pan; cover and keep warm.

2. Meanwhile, in a very large skillet heat olive oil over medium heat. Add chicken; cook for 8 to 12 minutes or until chicken is no longer pink (170°F), turning once. Remove chicken from skillet; discard pan drippings.

3. In the same skillet melt butter over medium heat. Add garlic; cook and stir for 15 seconds. Stir in artichokes, wine, the ¼ cup pistachio nuts, and the salt. Bring to boiling; reduce heat. Simmer, uncovered, for 5 minutes. Return chicken to skillet. Cook for 1 to 2 minutes or until heated through. Transfer chicken to a cutting board; cut diagonally into thin slices.

4. Arrange cooked pasta on dinner plates or a large serving platter; top with chicken. Spoon artichoke mixture over chicken and pasta. Sprinkle with parsley, additional pistachio nuts, pepper, and Parmesan cheese, if desired.

FOR 4 SERVINGS: Prepare using method above, except in Step 3 use the 2 tablespoons pistachio nuts.

PER SERVING *583 cal., 25 g total fat (8 g sat. fat), 82 mg chol., 325 mg sodium, 51 g carbo., 6 g fiber, 31 g pro.*

Garlic Chicken Stir-Fry

If you don't have a wok, use your largest skillet for stir-frying this incredible collection of Asian-style ingredients. The mixture is sensational on any variety of rice. Just remove the cooked rice from heat and let stand—with lid on, no peeking—for five minutes to make rice extra fluffy.

1. Cut chicken into ½-inch pieces. Place chicken in a resealable plastic bag set in a shallow dish. For marinade, stir together water, soy sauce, and vinegar. Pour over chicken; seal bag. Marinate in the refrigerator for 30 minutes. Drain chicken, reserving the marinade. Stir cornstarch into reserved marinade; set aside.

2. Pour oil into a wok or large skillet. (If necessary, add more oil during cooking.) Heat over medium-high heat. Add green onion slices, mushrooms, and garlic to wok; cook and stir for 1 to 2 minutes or until tender. Remove vegetables from wok.

3. Add chicken to wok; cook and stir for 2 to 3 minutes or until no longer pink. Push chicken from center of wok. Stir marinade mixture; add to center of wok. Cook and stir until thickened and bubbly. Return cooked vegetables to wok. Add water chestnuts. Cook and stir about 1 minute more or until heated through. If desired, sprinkle with chopped green onion. Serve with rice.

PER SERVING *311 cal., 8 g total fat (1 g sat. fat), 49 mg chol., 755 mg sodium, 35 g carbo., 2 g fiber, 25 g pro.*

PREP: 25 minutes
MARINATE: 30 minutes
COOK: 6 minutes

8 servings	ingredients	4 servings
24 oz.	skinless, boneless chicken breast halves	12 oz.
2 cups	water	1 cup
6 Tbsp.	reduced-sodium soy sauce	3 Tbsp.
2 Tbsp.	rice vinegar or white wine vinegar	1 Tbsp.
2 Tbsp.	cornstarch	1 Tbsp.
4 Tbsp.	vegetable oil	2 Tbsp.
20	green onions, bias-sliced into 1-inch pieces	10
2 cups	thinly sliced fresh mushrooms	1 cup
24 cloves	garlic, peeled and finely chopped	12 cloves
1 cup	sliced water chestnuts	½ cup
	Chopped green onion (optional)	
4 cups	hot cooked white, jasmine, or basmati rice	2 cups

Blackened Chicken with Avocado Salsa

The key to awesome avocado salsa is selecting a perfectly ripe, soft, and creamy avocado. To judge ripeness, try this trick: Flick your thumbnail across the little nub on the stem end. If it won't budge, the avocado is too green. If you can flick the stem nub off and see green beneath it, the avocado is perfectly ripe.

1. Preheat oven to 375°F. Lightly sprinkle both sides of each chicken breast half with blackened steak seasoning. In a large ovenproof skillet heat the 2 tablespoons oil over medium heat. Add chicken; cook until browned, turning once. Bake about 15 minutes or until the chicken is no longer pink (170°F).

2. For salsa, in a large bowl whisk together rice vinegar, the 4 tablespoons oil, the cumin, salt, and black pepper. Stir in avocado, papaya, sweet pepper, and chopped cilantro. Serve salsa with chicken. If desired, garnish with cilantro sprigs.

FOR 4 SERVINGS: Prepare using method above, except in Step 1 heat the 1 tablespoon oil over medium heat. In Step 2 use the 2 tablespoons oil.

PER SERVING *322 cal., 17 g total fat (3 g sat. fat), 82 mg chol., 513 mg sodium, 7 g carbo., 3 g fiber, 34 g pro.*

PREP: 20 minutes
BAKE: 15 minutes
OVEN: 375°F

8 servings	ingredients	4 servings
8	skinless, boneless chicken breast halves	4
4 tsp.	blackened steak seasoning	2 tsp.
2 Tbsp.	olive oil	1 Tbsp.
4 Tbsp.	rice vinegar	2 Tbsp.
4 Tbsp.	olive oil	2 Tbsp.
½ tsp.	ground cumin	¼ tsp.
¼ tsp.	salt	⅛ tsp.
⅛ tsp.	black pepper	dash
2	avocado, halved, seeded, peeled, and chopped	1
1⅓ cups	chopped fresh or refrigerated papaya	⅔ cup
⅔ cup	finely chopped red sweet pepper	⅓ cup
½ cup	chopped fresh cilantro	¼ cup
	Fresh cilantro sprigs (optional)	

Tomato-Apricot Chicken

If apricots and tomatoes sound like an unlikely combination, remember that tomatoes are actually a fruit—a fruit whose acidity plays well with the sweetness of dried apricots and raisins, creating a sweet-savory blend of flavors.

1. Season chicken with salt and pepper. Cook chicken in a very large skillet in hot oil for 4 minutes per side or until browned. Add garlic; cook and stir 1 minute more.

2. Add tomatoes, apricots, and raisins; bring to boiling. Reduce heat and simmer, covered, for 3 to 5 minutes or until chicken is cooked through (no pink remains). Uncover and cook to desired consistency. Season to taste with additional salt and pepper. If desired, sprinkle with snipped fresh parley and serve with cooked couscous.

PER SERVING *314 cal., 5 g total fat (1 g sat. fat), 82 mg chol., 636 mg sodium, 34 g carbo., 6 g fiber, 36 g pro.*

START TO FINISH: **25 minutes**

8 servings	ingredients	4 servings
8	boneless, skinless chicken breasts	4
	Salt	
	Black pepper	
1 Tbsp.	olive oil	1 Tbsp.
2 cloves	garlic, sliced	1 clove
2 28-oz. cans	diced tomatoes, undrained	1 28-oz. can
1 cup	snipped dried apricots	½ cup
⅔ cup	golden raisins	⅓ cup
	Snipped fresh parsley (optional)	
	Cooked couscous (optional)	

Chicken Lo Mein

Why call for Chinese takeout when you can prepare homemade lo mein in less than the normal delivery time? Because sesame oil may turn rancid quickly, keep it refrigerated.

1. Cut chicken into bite-size strips. In a medium bowl combine 4 tablespoons of the soy sauce, the rice vinegar, and 4 teaspoons of the sugar. Add chicken; toss to coat. Let stand at room temperature for 20 minutes or cover and chill for 1 hour. Cook noodles according to package directions until tender; drain. Rinse with cold water; drain well. Set noodles aside. For sauce, in a small bowl stir together chicken broth, the remaining 8 tablespoons soy sauce, the remaining 4 teaspoons sugar, and the cornstarch. Set aside.

2. Pour vegetable oil and sesame oil into a wok or large nonstick skillet. Heat over medium-high heat. Add garlic; cook and stir for 30 seconds. Add carrot; cook and stir for 2 minutes. Add bok choy and green onions; cook and stir for 2 minutes more. Remove vegetables from wok.

3. Drain chicken, discarding marinade. Add chicken to wok (add more oil if necessary); cook and stir for 3 to 4 minutes or until no longer pink. Push chicken from center of wok. Stir sauce and add to center of wok. Cook and stir until thickened and bubbly. Add the cooked noodles and vegetables. Using two spatulas or wooden spoons, lightly toss the mixture until combined and heated through. Transfer to a serving platter. Serve immediately.

FOR 6 SERVINGS: Prepare using method above, except in Step 1 combine 2 tablespoons of the soy sauce with the rice vinegar and 2 teaspoons of the sugar. For the sauce, use the remaining 4 tablespoons soy sauce and the remaining 2 teaspoons sugar.

PER SERVING 326 cal., 7 g total fat (1 g sat. fat), 73 mg chol., 615 mg sodium, 42 g carbo., 2 g fiber, 22 g pro.

PREP: 35 minutes
STAND: 20 minutes
COOK: 10 minutes

12 servings	ingredients	6 servings
24 oz.	skinless, boneless chicken breast halves	12 oz.
¾ cup	reduced-sodium soy sauce	6 Tbsp.
2 Tbsp.	rice vinegar	1 Tbsp.
8 tsp.	sugar	4 tsp.
20 oz.	dried Chinese egg noodles or linguine	10 oz.
⅔ cup	reduced-sodium chicken broth	⅓ cup
4 tsp.	cornstarch	2 tsp.
2 Tbsp.	vegetable oil	1 Tbsp.
2 Tbsp.	sesame oil	1 Tbsp.
8 cloves	cloves garlic, minced	4 cloves
1 cup	shredded carrot	½ cup
2 cups	chopped bok choy	1 cup
8	green onions, cut into 2-inch julienne strips	4

Osso Bucco Chicken

Chicken thighs become silken and succulent when allowed to slowly braise in aromatic liquids. To skin thighs easily, just pop the thighs in them freezer for about 15 minutes before pulling the thick skin away with your fingers.

1. Preheat oven to 350°F. Add flour to a large resealable plastic bag. Add chicken; seal bag. Shake bag to coat chicken thighs with flour.

2. Heat oil in a 5- to 6-quart oven-going Dutch oven over medium-high heat. Add chicken and cook until lightly browned, about 4 minutes per side. Transfer chicken to a platter. Add carrots, onion, and celery to Dutch oven. Cook and stir until vegetables are browned. Add garlic; cook 1 minute more.

3. Stir in undrained tomatoes, chicken broth, vinegar, thyme, pepper, and bay leaf. Return chicken to Dutch oven and bring to boiling. Cover, transfer to oven, and bake for 40 minutes or until chicken is done and vegetables are tender, carefully removing lid and stirring halfway through. Remove and discard bay leaf. Serve with Orange Gremolata.

ORANGE GREMOLATA: In a medium bowl combine 4 tablespoons finely chopped fresh parsley, 2 tablespoons minced garlic, 2 teaspoons finely shredded orange peel, 2 teaspoons vegetable oil, and 1/8 teaspoon each salt and black pepper.

PER SERVING 320 cal., 14 g total fat (2 g sat. fat), 115 mg chol., 632 mg sodium, 18 g carbo., 4 g fiber, 30 g pro.

PREP: 30 minutes
BAKE: 40 minutes
OVEN: 350°F

8 servings	ingredients	4 servings
¼ cup	all-purpose flour	2 Tbsp.
8	chicken thighs, skinned	4
2 Tbsp.	vegetable oil	1 Tbsp.
2 cups	sliced carrots	1 cup
1 cup	chopped onion	½ cup
1 cup	chopped celery	½ cup
2 cloves	garlic, minced	1 clove
2 14.5-oz. cans	diced tomatoes	1 14.5-oz. can
2 cup	chicken broth	1 cup
4 Tbsp.	red wine vinegar	2 Tbsp.
½ tsp.	dried thyme, crushed	¼ tsp.
½ tsp.	black pepper	¼ tsp.
2	bay leaves	1
1 recipe	Orange Gremolata	½ recipe

Curried Chicken Stew

Many of the world's most wonderful dishes are slowly braised—and braising is exactly what the slow cooker does, cooking chicken into succulent chunks of flavorful goodness. Serve this curry over aromatic jasmine or basmati rice.

PREP: 20 minutes
SLOW COOK: 7 hours (low) or 3½ hours (high)

8 servings	ingredients	4 servings
16	bone-in chicken thighs	8
4 tsp.	olive oil	2 tsp.
12	carrots, cut into 2-inch pieces	6
2 medium	sweet onion, cut into thin wedges	1 medium
2 cups	unsweetened coconut milk	1 cup
½ cup	mild or hot curry paste	¼ cup
	Chopped pistachios, golden raisins, cilantro, and/or crushed red pepper (optional)	

1. Trim excess skin and fat from chicken thighs (or remove skin if desired). In a very large skillet cook chicken, skin sides down, in hot olive oil for 8 minutes, or until browned. (Do not turn thighs.) Remove from heat; drain and discard fat.

2. In a 5- to 6-quart slow cooker combine carrots and onion wedges. In a bowl whisk together half the coconut milk and the curry paste; pour over carrots and onion (refrigerate remaining coconut milk). Place chicken, skin side up, on vegetables. Cover and cook on low for 7 to 8 hours or on high for 3½ to 4 hours.

3. Remove chicken from slow cooker. Skim off excess fat from sauce in cooker, then stir in remaining coconut milk.

4. Serve stew in bowls. Top each serving with pistachios, raisins, cilantro, and/or crushed red pepper.

FOR 4 SERVINGS: Prepare using method above, except in Step 2 use a 3½- or 4-quart slow cooker.

PER SERVING 850 cal., 63 g total fat (25 g sat. fat), 238 mg chol., 1,314 mg sodium, 21 g carbo., 5 g fiber, 52 g pro.

Jerk Chicken and Slaw

If the old adage "We eat with our eyes" is true, just the sight of this bright and beautiful dish will make mouths water. To select a ripe, juicy pineapple, look for even golden color, bright green leaves, and fresh, sweet aroma.

1. For pineapple slaw, in a very large bowl combine bok choy, cabbage, and pineapple. In a small bowl combine cider vinegar and 4 teaspoons of the brown sugar. Drizzle over slaw; toss to coat. Set aside.

2. In a large resealable plastic bag combine the remaining 4 teaspoons brown sugar, the flour, and jerk seasoning. Add chicken; shake well to coat. On a lightly greased grill pan or in a very large heavy skillet cook chicken over medium heat for 6 to 8 minutes or until no longer pink (170°F). Transfer chicken to a cutting board.

3. Slice chicken. Serve chicken with pineapple slaw.

FOR 4 SERVINGS: Prepare using method above, except in Step 1 use 2 teaspoons of the brown sugar and in Step 2 use the remaining 2 teaspoons.

PER SERVING *205 cal., 2 g total fat (0 g sat. fat), 66 mg chol., 318 mg sodium, 19 g carbo., 3 g fiber, 29 g pro.*

START TO FINISH: **25 minutes**

8 servings	ingredients	4 servings
6 heads	baby bok choy, trimmed and thinly sliced	3 heads
4 cups	shredded red cabbage	2 cups
1	peeled, cored fresh pineapple, chopped	½
4 Tbsp.	cider vinegar	2 Tbsp.
8 tsp.	packed brown sugar	4 tsp.
4 tsp.	all-purpose flour	2 tsp.
4 tsp.	jerk seasoning	2 tsp.
8	skinless, boneless chicken breast halves	4

Roasted Chicken, Focaccia, and Olive Salad

Thrifty Italian cooks often use the last bits of their artisan breads to make salad called panzanella. You'll love the way day-old focaccia absorbs the tangy dressing, making an incredibly flavorful blend.

START TO FINISH: **30 minutes**

8 servings	ingredients	4 servings
⅔ cup	olive oil	5 Tbsp.
½ cup	white wine or cider vinegar	¼ cup
4 tsp.	Mediterranean seasoning blend or spaghetti seasoning	2 tsp.
2 tsp.	sugar	1 tsp.
6 cups	torn, day-old garlic focaccia or Italian bread	3 cups
4 cups	shredded deli-roasted chicken	2 cups
1½ cups	pitted olives	¾ cup
6	romaine hearts, cored and coarsely chopped	3

1. For dressing, in a small bowl whisk together 8 tablespoons of the olive oil, the vinegar, seasoning blend, and sugar; set aside.

2. In a very large skillet heat 1 tablespoon oil over medium-high heat. Add bread. Cook and stir for 5 minutes until lightly toasted. Remove from skillet. Add dressing, chicken, and olives to skillet; cook and stir 2 to 3 minutes until chicken is heated through. Return bread to skillet; toss to coat.

3. Arrange lettuce on 8 plates; top with chicken mixture. Serve immediately.

FOR 4 SERVINGS: Prepare using method above, except in Step 1 use 4 tablespoons of the oil. In Step 2 heat 1 tablespoon oil. In Step 3 use 4 plates.

PER SERVING *478 cal., 34 g total fat (8 g sat. fat), 83 mg chol., 998 mg sodium, 22 g carbo., 3 g fiber, 21 g pro.*

Buffalo Chicken Salad

Warm marinated chicken over cool, crisp greens makes a perfect after-work supper. If your family likes it spicy, add a few more drops of hot pepper sauce.

1. For dressing, in a small bowl combine mayonnaise, barbecue sauce, blue cheese, milk, and 2 teaspoons hot pepper sauce.

2. Place chicken in a resealable plastic bag set in a shallow dish. Add ⅔ cup of the dressing and 1 teaspoon hot pepper sauce. Seal bag, turning to coat chicken. Marinate in the refrigerator for 30 minutes.

3. Preheat broiler. Drain chicken, discarding the marinade. Place chicken on the unheated rack of a broiler pan. Broil 4 to 5 inches from heat for 8 minutes. Turn chicken and broil 6 minutes more or until chicken is no longer pink (170°F).

4. Meanwhile, in a large bowl toss together lettuces, celery, and carrot sticks. Add remaining dressing to greens in bowl. Cut chicken into thin slices. Place on salad. Sprinkle with cheese.

FOR 6 SERVINGS: Prepare using method above, except in Step 1 use 1 teaspoon hot pepper sauce. In Step 2 add ⅓ cup of the dressing and ½ teaspoon hot pepper sauce.

PER SERVING 318 cal., 22 g total fat (6 g sat. fat), 76 mg chol., 488 mg sodium, 6 g carbo., 2 g fiber, 24 g pro.

PREP: 20 minutes
MARINATE: 30 minutes
BROIL: 14 minutes

12 servings	ingredients	6 servings
1 cup	mayonnaise	½ cup
½ cup	bottled barbecue sauce	¼ cup
1 cup (6 oz.)	crumbled blue cheese	½ cup (3 oz.)
4 Tbsp.	milk	2 Tbsp.
2 tsp.	bottled hot pepper sauce	1 tsp.
2½ lb.	skinless, boneless chicken breast halves	1¼ lb.
1 tsp.	bottled hot pepper sauce	½ tsp.
8 cups	torn iceberg lettuce	4 cups
6 cups	torn romaine lettuce	3 cups
4 stalks	celery, cut into 1- to 2-inch-long matchsticks	2 stalks
2	carrot, peeled and cut into 2-inch-long matchsticks	1
2 Tbsp.	crumbled blue cheese	1 Tbsp.

Southwestern Chicken Panini

Make this sandwich even simpler by relying on deli-roasted chicken for the shredded meat. Pulling and shredding the chicken is easier when the chicken is still warm. Reserve extra chicken for sandwiches and soups.

PREP: 30 minutes
COOK: 3 minutes per batch

8 servings	ingredients	4 servings
1 cup	chopped onion	½ cup
6 Tbsp.	olive oil	3 Tbsp.
1 cup	red enchilada sauce	½ cup
½ cup	pine nuts	¼ cup
4 Tbsp.	golden raisins	2 Tbsp.
3 tsp.	finely chopped chipotle chile in adobo sauce plus 1 tsp. adobo sauce*	1½ tsp.
3 tsp.	packed brown sugar	1½ tsp.
3 tsp.	white wine vinegar	1½ tsp.
½ tsp.	ground cinnamon	¼ tsp.
4 cups	shredded cooked chicken	2 cups
16	½-inch slices Italian country-style bread	8
2 cups	shredded Colby and/or Monterey jack cheese	1 cup
1 recipe	Mango Slaw	½ recipe

1. In a large skillet cook onion in 1 tablespoon hot oil for 3 to 4 minutes until softened. Stir in enchilada sauce, pine nuts, raisins, chipotle chile and sauce, brown sugar, vinegar, and cinnamon. Stir in chicken; heat through.

2. Preheat panini press or cast-iron skillet. Brush one side of 8 bread slices with some of the remaining oil. Turn over; place about ½ cup filling on each. Top with ¼ cup cheese and remaining 8 bread slices; brush with oil.

3. Place sandwich(es) in panini press and cook for 3 to 5 minutes or until bread is golden and cheese is melted. If using a skillet, toast both sides until golden. Serve with Mango Slaw.

MANGO SLAW: In a large bowl whisk together 4 tablespoons olive oil and 2 tablespoons lime juice. Add 4 cups finely shredded cabbage, 1 cup chopped mango, 4 tablespoons chopped cilantro, and salt and black pepper to taste. Toss to combine.

FOR 4 SERVINGS: Prepare using method above, except in Step 1 cook onion in 1 tablespoon hot oil. In Step 2 brush one side of 4 bread slices with some of the remaining oil. Turn over; place about ½ cup filling on each. Top with ¼ cup cheese and remaining 4 bread slices.

PER SERVING 663 cal., 37 g total fat (10 g sat. fat), 86 mg chol., 941 mg sodium, 47 g carbo., 4 g fiber, 36 g pro.

*NOTE: Because chile peppers contain volatile oils that can burn your skin and eyes, avoid direct contact with them as much as possible. When working with chile peppers, wear plastic or rubber gloves. If your bare hands do touch the peppers, wash your hands and nails well with soap and warm water.

Grilled Chicken Salad

Pine nuts toast quickly. The quickest and safest way is to place the nuts in a skillet over medium heat, then shake the skillet just until the kernels turn golden and exude a toasty aroma. Remove the skillet from heat immediately to stop the cooking.

PREP: 20 minutes
STAND: 1 hour
GRILL: 12 minutes

8 servings	ingredients	4 servings
½ cup	grape seed oil or olive oil	¼ cup
6 Tbsp.	balsamic vinegar	3 Tbsp.
2 Tbsp.	dried dillweed	1 Tbsp.
2 cloves	garlic, minced	1 clove
½ tsp.	freshly ground black pepper	¼ tsp.
½ tsp.	dried oregano, crushed	¼ tsp.
8	skinless, boneless chicken breast halves	4
	Montreal steak seasoning or Kansas City steak seasoning	
16 cups	mesclun or spring salad greens or spinach	8 cups
1½ cups	seedless red grapes, halved	¾ cup
⅔ cup	crumbled goat cheese	⅓ cup
½ cup	pine nuts, toasted	¼ cup

1. For vinaigrette, in a screw-top jar combine oil, vinegar, dillweed, garlic, pepper, and oregano. Cover and shake well; let stand 1 hour.

2. Meanwhile, sprinkle chicken breast halves lightly with steak seasoning. Grill chicken on the rack of an uncovered grill directly over medium coals for 12 to 15 minutes or until tender and no longer pink (170°F), turning once. Cool slightly.

3. Arrange salad greens on 8 plates. Slice each chicken breast and arrange 1 sliced breast on each salad. Top with grapes, goat cheese, and pine nuts. Shake dressing and drizzle over the greens.

FOR 4 SERVINGS: Prepare using method above, except in Step 3 use 4 plates.

PER SERVING 400 cal., 23 g total fat (4 g sat. fat), 86 mg chol., 167 mg sodium, 12 g carbo., 2 g fiber, 38 g pro.

Asian Chicken and Rice Salad

Some canned baby corn may have a hint of metallic taste. Sample the corn to taste. If you detect an off taste, all it takes to renew the fresh flavor is to give the little cobs a 2-minute bath in boiling water. Drain well before using.

1. Cook rice mix according to package directions.

2. Meanwhile, in a large bowl combine chicken, corn, sweet pepper, pea pods, and green onions. Stir in cooked rice. Add dressing; stir gently to combine.

3. If desired, sprinkle salad with sesame seeds.

MAKE-AHEAD DIRECTIONS: Prepare salad as directed through Step 2. Cover and chill for up to 24 hours. If desired, sprinkle with sesame seeds before serving.

PER SERVING *429 cal., 14 g total fat (3 g sat. fat), 62 mg chol., 1,057 mg sodium, 46 g carbo., 5 g fiber, 26 g pro.*

START TO FINISH: **25 minutes**

8 servings	ingredients	4 servings
2 6- to 7-oz. pkg.	rice pilaf mix	1 6- to 7-oz. pkg.
4 cups	shredded or chopped cooked chicken	2 cups
2 14-oz. cans	whole baby corn, drained	1 14-oz. can
1 cup	chopped red sweet pepper	½ cup
1 cup	fresh snow pea pods, sliced, or thinly sliced celery	½ cup
½ cup	sliced green onions	¼ cup
1 cup	bottled Asian salad dressing	½ cup
	Toasted sesame seeds (optional)	

Pulled Chicken-Peanut Salad

Grown-ups will appreciate this quick and easy Asian-style salad, but its most enthusiastic customers might be kids. Children love itty-bitty mandarin oranges, adore peanuts, and feel friendly toward chicken—this healthful salad is bound to be a pint-size favorite.

1. For dressing, in a small bowl stir together juice concentrate, water, sesame oil, salt, and pepper. Set aside.

2. Arrange greens on salad plates. Top with chicken, oranges, and peanuts. Drizzle with dressing.

PER SERVING *263 cal., 12 g total fat (3 g sat. fat), 62 mg chol., 247 mg sodium, 15 g carbo., 2 g fiber, 24 g pro.*

START TO FINISH: **25 minutes**

8 servings	ingredients	4 servings
4 Tbsp.	frozen orange juice concentrate, thawed	2 Tbsp.
2 Tbsp.	water	1 Tbsp.
4 tsp.	toasted sesame oil	2 tsp.
½ tsp.	salt	¼ tsp.
¼ tsp.	coarsely ground black pepper	⅛ tsp.
12 cups	torn mixed salad greens	6 cups
4 cups	coarsely shredded cooked chicken	2 cups
2 11-oz. cans	mandarin orange sections, drained	1 11-oz. can
½ cup	dry-roasted peanuts	¼ cup

Pesto Chicken Salad

Deli-roasted chicken makes quick work of this substantial main-dish salad. Dried tomato pesto is usually located in the produce department, alongside basil pesto, jarred minced garlic, and chopped ginger.

1. Remove and shred enough meat from the chicken to equal 4 cups. Save any remaining chicken for another use.

2. In a large skillet cook mushrooms in hot oil over medium heat about 10 minutes or until tender, stirring occasionally. Stir in pesto and vinegar. Bring to boiling. Stir in chopped chicken; heat through. Gently stir in tomatoes.

3. Line a serving platter with salad greens; top with chicken mixture. Serve warm.

FOR 4 SERVINGS: Prepare using method above, except in Step 1 remove enough meat from the chicken to equal 2 cups.

PER SERVING *419 cal., 24 g total fat (6 g sat. fat), 96 mg chol., 330 mg sodium, 14 g carbo., 3 g fiber, 38 g pro.*

START TO FINISH: **30 minutes**

8 servings	ingredients	4 servings
2 2- to 2¼-lb.	purchased roasted chicken	1 2- to 2¼-lb.
16 oz.	sliced fresh mushrooms	8 oz.
4 Tbsp.	olive oil	2 Tbsp.
1 cup	dried tomato pesto	½ cup
6 Tbsp.	balsamic vinegar	3 Tbsp.
1 cup	cherry tomatoes, halved	½ cup
16 cups	mixed salad greens	8 cups

Layered Turkey Enchiladas

Latin Lasagna might be another name for this recipe—it's filled with ooey-gooey layers of goodness. If you'd like to add a little more pizzazz, shred jalapeño-studded pepper Jack cheese instead of using the Mexican-blend cheese.

1. Position oven rack toward top of oven. Preheat oven to 450°F. In an extra-large skillet cook turkey in hot oil over medium heat for 4 minutes or until no longer pink. Add frozen vegetables, enchilada sauce, and cranberry sauce. Bring to boiling. Sprinkle with salt and pepper.

2. In each of two 2-quart baking dishes layer one-third of the tortillas, then one-third of the cheese. Use a slotted spoon to layer half the turkey-vegetable mixture. Layer one-third tortillas, one-third cheese, remaining turkey-vegetables (with slotted spoon), and remaining tortillas. Spoon on remaining sauce from skillet; sprinkle with remaining cheese. Bake 15 minutes or until cheese is melted. Cut into squares. If desired, serve with lime and cilantro.

FOR 4 SERVINGS: Prepare using method above, except in Step 2 use one 2-quart baking dish.

PER SERVING 615 cal., 25 g total fat (11 g sat. fat), 120 mg chol., 1,171 mg sodium, 52 g carbo., 6 g fiber, 45 g pro.

COOK: 4 minutes
BAKE: 15 minutes
OVEN: 450°F

8 servings	ingredients	4 serving
2 lb.	turkey breast tenderloin, cut in bite-size strips	1 lb.
2 Tbsp.	vegetable oil	1 Tbsp.
2 16-oz. pkg.	frozen sweet peppers and onions stir-fry vegetables	1 16-oz. pkg.
2 10-oz. cans	enchilada sauce	1 10-oz. can
1 cup	whole berry cranberry sauce	½ cup
	Salt and black pepper	
18 6-inch	corn tortillas, halved	9 6-inch
2 8-oz. pkg. (4 cups)	Mexican-blend shredded cheese	1 8-oz. pkg. (2 cups)
	Lime wedges (optional)	
	Fresh cilantro sprigs (optional)	

Cajun Turkey Cutlets with Fresh Melon Salsa

START TO FINISH: **18 minutes**

8 servings	ingredients	4 servings
4 1- to 1½-lb.	turkey breast tenderloins	2 1- to 1½-lb.
2 Tbsp.	olive oil	1 Tbsp.
1 Tbsp.	Cajun seasoning	1½ tsp.
12 cups	torn mixed greens	6 cups
3 cups	sliced cantaloupe	1½ cups
2 cups	fresh blueberries	1 cup
	Crumbled farmer's cheese (optional)	
	Purchased salad dressing of your choice	

With this recipe, a fresh and fabulous summer dinner will be yours in less than 20 minutes. If you'd like, substitute honeydew or Crenshaw melons in the cooling, juicy salsa—they're just as delicious.

1. Cut each turkey tenderloin in half horizontally to make 8 steaks. Brush turkey pieces with olive oil. Sprinkle with Cajun seasoning.

2. For a charcoal grill, grill turkey on the rack of an uncovered grill directly over medium coals for 12 to 15 minutes or until turkey is no longer pink (170°F), turning once halfway through grilling. (For a gas grill, preheat grill. Reduce heat to medium. Place turkey on grill rack over heat. Cover and grill as above.) Slice turkey.

3. Arrange greens on a large serving platter or 8 dinner plates. Arrange turkey, cantaloupe, and berries on greens. If desired, sprinkle with cheese. Pass desired dressing.

FOR 4 SERVINGS: Prepare using method above, except in Step 1 cut tenderloins to make 4 steaks. In Step 3 arrange greens on a serving platter or 4 dinner plates.

PER SERVING *355 cal., 21 g total fat (4 g sat. fat), 70 mg chol., 145 mg sodium, 14 g carbo., 3 g fiber, 30 g pro.*

Turkey Pot Pie Casserole

Take Thanksgiving leftovers to flavorful new heights with this ingenious take on pot pie. No need to fuss with crust—thinly sliced apples, sage, and nutmeg caramelize on the tops, creating a crust like no other.

1. Preheat oven to 450°F. In a large microwave safe bowl combine vegetables, gravy, and fresh sage or ground sage. Cover with vented plastic wrap and cook on high for 5 minutes. Add turkey, cover, and cook 4 to 6 minutes more or until mixture is heated through and vegetables are tender, stirring occasionally.

2. In a small bowl combine pepper and nutmeg.

3. Spoon hot turkey mixture into eight 14- to 16-ounce individual casseroles. Top with sliced apple, and, if desired, fresh sage leaves. Drizzle with melted butter and sprinkle with the nutmeg mixture.

4. Bake, uncovered, for 10 minutes or until bubbly and apples are beginning to brown.

FOR 4 SERVINGS: Prepare using method above, except in Step 3 spoon hot turkey mixture into four 14- to 16-ounce individual casseroles.

PER SERVING *297 cal., 12 g total fat (5 g sat. fat), 71 mg chol., 753 mg sodium, 23 g carbo., 3 g fiber, 24 g pro.*

START TO FINISH: **25 minutes**
OVEN: **450°F**

8 servings	ingredients	4 servings
2 16-oz. bag	frozen stew vegetables (potatoes, carrots, onion, and celery)	1 16-oz. bag
2 18-oz. jars	home style gravy	1 18-oz. jar
2 tsp. or 1 tsp.	finely snipped fresh sage ground sage	1 tsp. or ½ tsp.
4 cups	cooked turkey, sliced	2 cups
½ tsp.	black pepper	¼ tsp.
½ tsp.	ground nutmeg	¼ tsp.
2	cooking apples, thinly sliced	1
	Fresh sage leaves (optional)	
2 Tbsp.	butter, melted	2 Tbsp.

Italian Meatball Rolls

PREP: 15 minutes
COOK: 12 minutes
BROIL: 2 minutes

8 servings	ingredients	4 servings
	Nonstick cooking spray	
5 cups	thinly sliced cremini mushrooms	2½ cups
1 cup	chopped onion	½ cup
4 cloves	garlic, minced	2 cloves
2 8-oz. cans	no-salt-added tomato sauce	1 8-oz. can
4 Tbsp.	balsamic vinegar	2 Tbsp.
1 tsp.	dried rosemary, crushed	½ tsp.
1 tsp.	dried oregano, crushed	½ tsp.
16 oz.	refrigerated Italian-style cooked turkey meatballs, halved	8 oz.
8	whole wheat hot dog buns	4
1 cup	shredded part-skim mozzarella cheese	½ cup
	Snipped fresh oregano (optional)	

Talk about a sandwich! This one—packed with mushrooms and lean turkey meatballs and slathered with balsamic-enriched sauce—will win raves at the table. Cremini mushrooms are just baby portobellos. If you cannot find them, slice some portobellos instead (discard the stems).

1. Preheat broiler. Coat a large nonstick skillet with nonstick spray; preheat over medium heat. Add mushrooms, onion, and garlic to hot skillet; cook for 5 to 10 minutes or until tender, stirring occasionally. Add tomato sauce, balsamic vinegar, rosemary, and dried oregano. Bring to boiling; reduce heat. Simmer, covered, for 2 minutes. Stir in meatballs. Cook about 5 minutes more or until meatballs are heated through.

2. Meanwhile, open buns flat and place on a baking sheet. Broil 4 to 5 inches from the heat about 1 minute or until lightly toasted. Divide meatball mixture among buns. Sprinkle with cheese. Broil for 1 to 2 minutes more or until cheese is melted. If desired, sprinkle with fresh oregano.

PER SERVING *344 cal., 12 g total fat (4 g sat. fat), 70 mg chol., 644 mg sodium, 36 g carbo., 4 g fiber, 21 g pro.*

Turkey Dinner Burgers

Jalapeño pepper jelly adds an enticing zip to broiled turkey burgers. Select ground turkey or chicken packaged in open, clear-wrapped meat packaging—ground meats that come in tubes tend to be too finely ground for juicy burgers.

PREP: 15 minutes
BROIL: 14 minutes

8 servings	ingredients	4 servings
2	eggs, lightly beaten	1
1 tsp.	salt	½ tsp.
½ tsp.	black pepper	¼ tsp.
2 lbs.	uncooked lean ground turkey or ground chicken	1 lb.
½ cup	fine dry bread crumbs	¼ cup
2 Tbsp.	olive oil	1 Tbsp.
½ cup	jalapeño pepper jelly, melted	¼ cup
	Shredded red cabbage, thinly sliced red onion, and/or other desired toppings	
8	ciabatta rolls, potato rolls, Kaiser rolls, or hamburger buns, split and toasted	4

1. In a large bowl combine egg, salt, and pepper. Add turkey and bread crumbs; mix well. Shape the poultry mixture into eight ¾-inch-thick patties.

2. Place patties on the unheated rack of a broiler pan. Broil 4 to 5 inches from the heat for 12 to 14 minutes or until an instant-read thermometer inserted into the thickest part of the burger registers 165°F, turning once halfway through cooking time. Brush patties with half of the jalapeño jelly. Broil 1 minute; turn and brush with remaining jelly. Broil 1 minute more.

3. To assemble, place cabbage, red onion, and/or other desired toppings on bottoms of rolls; top with patties and roll tops.

FOR 4 SERVINGS: Prepare using method above, except in Step 1 shape poultry mixture into four ¾-inch-thick patties

PER SERVING 504 cal., 20 g total fat (2 g sat. fat), 55 mg chol., 900 mg sodium, 52 g carbo., 2 g fiber, 28 g pro.

Grilled Fajita Burgers

Perch these spicy, salsa-seasoned burgers and their tender-crisp onions and peppers on a corn tostada shell to create a lean and lovely twist on the traditional two-bun burger.

1. In a medium bowl combine turkey, salsa, cumin, black pepper, and salt. Mix well. Shape into four ½-inch-thick patties. Fold a 24×12-inch piece of heavy-duty foil in half to make a 12-inch square. Place onion and sweet pepper in center of foil; drizzle with oil. Bring up two opposite edges of foil and seal with a double fold. Fold remaining edges together to completely enclose the vegetables, leaving space for steam to build.*

2. For a charcoal grill place vegetable packet and patties on the rack of an uncovered grill directly over medium heat. Grill for 10 to 13 minutes or until an instant-read thermometer inserted into the side of each patty registers 165°F for turkey or 160°F for beef and vegetables are tender, turning once halfway through grilling. (For a gas grill preheat grill. Reduce heat to medium. Place packet and patties on grill rack over heat. Cover and grill as above.)

3. Serve patties on tostada shells. Top with vegetables and avocado.

FOR 2 SERVINGS: Prepare using method above, except in Step 1 shape into two ½-inch-thick patties.

*NOTE: The pepper slices and onion mixture may be cooked in a skillet on the side burner of the grill or on the range top. In a covered medium skillet cook onion and red pepper slices in hot oil over medium heat for 10 minutes, stirring occasionally. Uncover and cook about 3 minutes more or until pepper is very tender and onion is golden brown, stirring occasionally.

PER SERVING *285 cal., 10 g total fat (1 g sat. fat), 55 mg chol., 430 mg sodium, 20 g carbo., 5 g fiber, 29 g pro.*

PREP: 20 minutes
GRILL: 10 minutes

4 servings	ingredients	2 servings
16 oz.	uncooked ground turkey breast or 90% or higher lean ground beef	8 oz.
½ cup	purchased salsa	¼ cup
½ tsp.	ground cumin	¼ tsp.
¼ tsp.	black pepper	⅛ tsp.
	Dash salt	
1 cup	thinly sliced sweet onion (such as Vidalia or Maui Maui)	½ cup
1 (1 cup)	medium red sweet pepper, thinly sliced	½ (½ cup)
2 tsp.	canola oil	1 tsp.
4	purchased tostada shells	2
½	medium avocado, seeded, peeled, and sliced or chopped	¼

CHAPTER 3

Meat

For substantial, stick-to-the-ribs recipes for beef, ham, pork, and sausage—from stews to sandwiches—turn the page and dig right in. Whether you eat meat several nights a week or just occasionally, you can make it the star of the meal every time.

79

91

102

Peppered Steaks with Roasted Beets

Select beets no larger than a golf ball when preparing the earthy, sweet topping for these juicy sirloins. Offset the beef's delectable richness by serving with baby salad greens tossed in light, lemony vinaigrette.

1. Trim and reserve beet greens; set aside. Peel beets; cut into wedges. Place in a 3-quart microwave-safe dish. Cover with vented plastic wrap. Cook on high for 9 to 12 minutes until tender, stirring once. Rinse and drain greens; tear to measure 2 cups; set aside. Carefully uncover and drain beets. Toss with olive oil, ¼ teaspoon of the salt, the ¼ teaspoon black pepper, and torn greens.

2. Meanwhile, season both sides of steak with the remaining ½ teaspoon salt and 2 teaspoons cracked black pepper. Lightly coat grill pan or cast-iron skillet with nonstick cooking spray. Heat over medium-high heat. Cook steak for 5 minutes per side or to desired doneness. For sauce, in a small saucepan stir together the water, the mustard, and brown sugar over medium heat just until bubbly.

3. Cut steak into 8 portions, then top with beets and sauce. Combine cream cheese and seasoning; spoon over steak, beets, and sauce.

FOR 4 SERVINGS: Prepare using method above, except in Step 1 use a 1½-quart microwave safe dish. Tear greens to measure 1 cup. Toss with 1 tablespoon olive oil and ⅛ teaspoon salt and a dash of black pepper. In Step 2 season both sides of steak with ¼ teaspoon salt and 1 teaspoon cracked black pepper. For the sauce, use 2 tablespoons water. In Step 3 cut the steak into 4 portions.

PER SERVING *418 cal., 27 g total fat (11 g sat. fat), 83 mg chol., 418 mg sodium, 17 g carbo., 4 g fiber, 27 g pro.*

START TO FINISH: **30 minutes**

8 servings	ingredients	4 servings
4 lb.	small golden and/or red beets with tops	2 lb.
2 Tbsp.	Olive oil	1 Tbsp.
¾ tsp.	salt	¼ tsp.
¼ tsp.	black pepper	⅛ tsp.
2 lb.	boneless beef sirloin steak, 1 inch thick	1 lb.
	Nonstick cooking spray	
2 tsp.	cracked black pepper	1 tsp.
¼ cup	water	2 Tbsp.
2 Tbsp.	deli-style mustard	1 Tbsp.
2 tsp.	packed brown sugar	1 tsp.
1 8-oz. pkg.	cream cheese, softened	½ 8-oz. pkg.
1 tsp.	dried Italian seasoning	½ tsp.

Beef Tips with Smoky Pepper Sauce

If you haven't tried smoked paprika yet, give it a try. Made by smoking, drying, and grinding red sweet bell peppers into a fine powder, the product adds a wonderful smoky sweet-taste to all sorts of dishes.

1. Trim fat from meat; cut meat into 1- to 1½-inch pieces. Sprinkle meat with paprika. In a very large skillet heat oil over medium-high heat. Add meat to skillet; cook for 5 minutes or to desired doneness. Remove meat from skillet.

2. Meanwhile, drain roasted peppers, reserving liquid. Coarsely chop the peppers. Measure 1 cup of the reserved liquid (if necessary, add enough water to equal 1 cup).

3. Add peppers and the liquid to the skillet. Stir in barbecue sauce. Cook, uncovered, for 5 to 10 minutes or until sauce is slightly thickened, stirring frequently. Return meat to skillet; heat through. Sprinkle with parsley. If desired, serve with polenta.

FOR 4 SERVINGS: Prepare using method above, except in Step 2 measure ½ cup of the reserved liquid (if necessary, add enough water to equal ½ cup).

PER SERVING *367 cal., 18 g total fat (6 g sat. fat), 111 mg chol., 510 mg sodium, 13 g carbo., 2 g fiber, 36 g pro.*

START TO FINISH: **30 minutes**

8 servings	ingredients	4 servings
3 lb.	beef sirloin tip steak	1½ lb.
1 tsp.	smoked paprika or paprika	½ tsp.
2 Tbsp.	vegetable oil	1 Tbsp.
2 12- to 16-oz. jars	roasted red and/or yellow sweet peppers	1 12- to 16-oz. jar
1 cup	hickory- or mesquite-flavor barbecue sauce	½ cup
½ cup	coarsely chopped fresh parsley	¼ cup
	Cooked polenta (optional)	

Beef with Mushrooms and Pearl Onions

These top loin steaks take on the flavor of classic French Beef Burgundy, making them an aromatic dish perfect for company. Dry red wines that bring the most flavor to this dish include Burgundy, Cabernet Sauvignon, and Shiraz.

1. Trim fat from steaks. Cut steaks in half. Sprinkle steaks with the pepper and salt. Preheat a very large skillet over medium-high heat. Add oil; swirl to lightly coat skillet. Reduce heat to medium. Add steaks; cook for 8 to 10 minutes or until medium-rare (145°F), turning once. Transfer steaks to a tray or plate; cover with foil and let stand while preparing sauce.

2. For sauce, in the same skillet cook mushrooms and onions over medium-high heat about 5 minutes or until tender, stirring frequently. Add garlic. Cook for 1 minute more. Remove skillet from heat; add wine. Return skillet to heat. Boil gently, uncovered, for 5 minutes, stirring occasionally. Whisk together broth and flour; add to skillet. Cook and stir until sauce is thickened and bubbly; cook and stir for 1 minute more.

3. Return steaks to skillet; heat through, turning to coat steaks evenly with sauce. Transfer steaks and sauce to serving plates. Sprinkle with parsley.

FOR 4 SERVINGS: Prepare using method above, except in Step 1 use a large skillet.

PER SERVING *287 cal., 11 g total fat (4 g sat. fat), 64 mg chol., 330 mg sodium, 11 g carbo., 2 g fiber, 28 g pro.*

START TO FINISH: **30 minutes**

8 servings	ingredients	4 servings
4 8-oz.	beef top loin steaks, cut ¾ to 1 inch thick	2 8-oz.
1 tsp.	cracked black pepper	½ tsp.
½ tsp.	salt	¼ tsp.
2 tsp.	olive oil	1 tsp.
16 oz.	fresh mushrooms, quartered	8 oz.
2 cups	frozen pearl onions	1 cup
8 cloves	garlic, minced	4 cloves
1½ cups	dry red wine	¾ cup
2 cups	lower-sodium beef broth	1 cup
¼ cup	whole wheat flour	2 Tbsp.
2 Tbsp.	snipped fresh parsley	1 Tbsp.

Beef and Carrot Ragu

Ragu—a thick, meat-filled sauce—is a hearty, full-bodied Italian classic. Enjoy the sumptuous slow-cooked mixture as is, like a stew, or feel free to ladle it over cooked penne or farfalle with a shaving of Parmesan cheese.

1. Trim excess fat from rib meat. Cut beef in chunks, then sprinkle lightly with salt and pepper. Place beef in a 5- to 6-quart slow cooker.

2. Smash garlic cloves with the flat side of a chef's knife or meat mallet. Separate and discard garlic skins. Place smashed garlic on beef. Add carrots and tomatoes to slow cooker.

3. In a medium bowl whisk together tomato paste and water or wine. Poor over meat and vegetables. Cover and cook on high for 3 to 4 hours or on low for 6 to 8 hours.

4. Stir well before serving. Top servings with basil leaves.

FOR 4 SERVINGS: Prepare using method above, except in Step 1 place beef in a 3½- or 4-quart slow cooker.

PER SERVING *509 cal., 42 g total fat (18 g sat. fat), 86 mg chol., 568 mg sodium, 15 g carbo., 4 g fiber, 19 g pro.*

PREP: 25 minutes
SLOW COOK: 3 hours (low) or 6 hours (high)

8 servings	ingredients	4 servings
2 to 3 lb.	boneless beef short ribs	1 to 1½ lb.
	Salt and black pepper	
20 cloves	garlic	10 cloves
2 8-oz. pkg.	peeled fresh baby carrots, chopped	1 8-oz. pkg.
2 lb.	plum tomatoes, chopped	1 lb.
1 6-oz. can	tomato paste with basil, garlic, and oregano	½ 6-oz. can
1 cup	water or red wine	½ cup
	Fresh basil leaves (optional)	

Beef Stew and Garlic Mash

This classic, high-end bistro dish comes together quickly and easily using convenience products. You'll love how easily garlic cloves peel when they have been steamed in the microwave.

1. In a 4-quart Dutch oven combine frozen vegetables and the ½ cup water. Bring to boiling. Meanwhile, microwave beef tips according to package directions.

2. Add beef tips and gravy and Worcestershire sauce to vegetables in Dutch oven. Bring to boiling; reduce heat. Simmer, covered, about 5 minutes or until vegetables are tender.

3. Meanwhile, in a small microwave-safe bowl place garlic and the ¼ cup water. Cover with vented plastic wrap. Cook on high for 1 minute; set aside. Place potatoes in a large microwave-safe bowl. Cook potatoes, uncovered, on high for 8 to 10 minutes or until tender, stirring once halfway through cooking.

4. For garlic mash, peel garlic; mash garlic with the back of a spoon. Add garlic, olive oil, salt, and pepper to potatoes. Mash with a potato masher or electric mixer on low. Divide garlic mash among 8 shallow bowls. Spoon beef mixture over garlic mash; sprinkle with oregano leaves.

FOR 4 SERVINGS: Prepare using method above, except in Step 1 use ¼ cup water. In Step 3 use 2 tablespoons water.

PER SERVING 368 cal., 14 g total fat (3 g sat. fat), 47 mg chol., 888 mg sodium, 42 g carbo., 8 g fiber, 24 g pro.

START TO FINISH: 25 minutes

8 servings	ingredients	4 servings
2 1-lb. pkg.	frozen assorted vegetable blend (carrots, peas, and onions)	1 1-lb. pkg.
½ cup	water	¼ cup
2 17-oz. pkg.	refrigerated cooked beef tips in gravy	1 17-oz. pkg.
4 tsp.	Worcestershire sauce	2 tsp.
12 cloves	garlic	6 cloves
¼ cup	water	2 Tbsp.
2 lb.	Yukon gold or red potatoes, halved	1 lb.
¼ cup	olive oil	2 Tbsp.
½ tsp.	salt	¼ tsp.
½ tsp.	freshly ground black pepper	¼ tsp.
¼ cup	fresh oregano leaves	2 Tbsp.

Mustard-Crusted Steaks with Herb Butter

Mark this recipe for any special dinner you have coming up—it makes for an indulgent, delicious feast. A rich steak such as this needs little accompaniment—steamed green beans or carrots would make a perfect side dish.

1. Preheat broiler. Cut each steak in half. Lightly sprinkle both sides of steaks with salt and black pepper.

2. In a large skillet heat 2 tablespoons of the butter over medium-high heat. Add steaks; brown on both sides, cooking until steaks are near desired doneness, about 3 to 4 minutes per side. Transfer to broiler pan; spread top of steaks with mustard.

3. Broil 3 to 4 inches from heat for 2 to 3 minutes or until steaks have reached desired doneness.

4. Meanwhile, for herb butter, add remaining butter to skillet; cook over medium heat until butter begins to bubble and turn golden. Add half the herbs; remove from heat.

5. Transfer steaks to plates; pour herb butter over steaks. Sprinkle with remaining herbs.

FOR 4 SERVINGS: Prepare using method above, except in Step 2 use 1 tablespoon of the butter.

PER SERVING *452 cal., 33 g total fat (16 g sat. fat), 110 mg chol., 496 mg sodium, 0 g carbo., 0 g fiber, 35 g pro.*

START TO FINISH: **30 minutes**

8 servings	ingredients	4 servings
4 12-oz.	boneless beef sirloin steaks, cut about ¾-inch thick	2 12-oz.
	Salt and black pepper	
½ cup	butter	¼ cup
¼ cup	coarse-grain mustard	2 Tbsp.
2 Tbsp.	snipped fresh thyme	1 Tbsp.
2 tsp.	snipped fresh rosemary	1 tsp.

Southwestern Meatball Chili

If you seldom use tomato paste, consider purchasing it in the clever squeezable tubes that allow you to extract just what you need. Or remove the paste from the can, transfer it to a nonmetal container, and refrigerate for up to two weeks.

1. In a Dutch oven combine thawed meatballs and vegetables, fresh tomatoes, the water, chili powder, and tomato paste. Cook, covered, over medium-low heat for 20 minutes, stirring occasionally.

2. Ladle chili into bowls. If desired, top with jalapeños, cherry tomatoes, and/or cilantro.

VARIATION: Substitute turkey meatballs for the beef meatballs. Substitute two 16-ounce packages frozen carrots, peas, and green beans for the Santa Fe vegetables (for 4 servings, use one 16-ounce package). Substitute 2 tablespoons Italian seasoning for the chili powder (for 4 servings, use 1 tablespoon).

PER SERVING *386 cal., 24 g total fat (11 g sat. fat), 93 mg chol., 944 mg sodium, 25 g carbo., 8 g fiber, 20 g pro.*

START TO FINISH: **25 minutes**

8 servings	ingredients	4 servings
2 14- to 16-oz. pkg.	fully cooked refrigerated or frozen beef meatballs, thawed	1 14- to 16-oz. pkg.
2 16-oz. pkg.	Santa Fe medley frozen mixed vegetables (corn, black beans, and red peppers)	1 16-oz. pkg.
4 cups	chopped fresh tomatoes and/or cherry tomatoes	2 cups
3 cups	water	1½ cups
2 Tbsp.	chili powder	1 Tbsp.
6 Tbsp.	tomato paste	3 Tbsp.
	Sliced jalapeño peppers (see note, page 54), chopped cherry tomatoes, and/or fresh cilantro (optional)	

Grilled Panini Burgers

Dry-cured capocolla—an Italian pork cold cut seasoned with wine, garlic, and Italian seasonings—is delicious served cold, but it's absolutely incredible when crisped, as it is in these panini.

1. In a large bowl combine ground beef, vinegar, tomato paste, garlic, and salt. Shape mixture into twelve 4-inch patties, about ½ inch thick. For a charcoal grill, grill patties on the rack of an uncovered grill directly over medium coals for 10 to 13 minutes or until an instant-read thermometer inserted into sides of patties registers 160°F, turning once and placing a mozzarella cheese slice on each patty for the last 1 minute of grilling. (For a gas grill, preheat grill. Reduce heat to medium. Place patties on grill rack over heat. Cover and grill as above.)

2. Meanwhile, in a small bowl combine semisoft cheese and mayonnaise. Spread onto cut sides of ciabatta rolls. Set aside. In a large bowl combine spinach, onion, and marinade.

3. Place a grilled patty on cheese spread on roll bottoms. Top with capocolla, tomato slices, and spinach mixture. Add roll tops, spread sides down. Place each sandwich on a piece of parchment paper or foil that is large enough to fold over the sandwich to cover the top.

4. Place the sandwiches, half at a time if needed, on the parchment or foil on the grill rack over medium-low coals or medium-low heat. Fold the parchment paper or foil up over tops of sandwiches. Place a foil-wrapped brick on sandwiches. Cover and grill 3 to 4 minutes or until bottoms of rolls are lightly toasted.

5. Unwrap sandwiches and serve warm.

FOR 6 SERVINGS: Prepare using method above, except in Step 1 shape beef into six 4-inch patties.

PER SERVING *840 cal., 57 g total fat (25 g sat. fat), 143 mg chol., 1,723 mg sodium, 36 g carbo., 3 g fiber, 45 g pro.*

START TO FINISH: **50 minutes**

12 servings	ingredients	6 servings
4 lb.	ground beef chuck	2 lb.
6 Tbsp.	balsamic vinegar	3 Tbsp.
4 Tbsp.	tomato paste	2 Tbsp.
6 cloves	garlic, minced	3 cloves
2 tsp.	salt	1 tsp.
12 slices	mozzarella cheese	6 slices
2 oz.	semisoft cheese with garlic and herbs	1 oz.
6 Tbsp.	mayonnaise	3 Tbsp.
12	ciabatta rolls, split and toasted	6
8 cups	fresh baby spinach leaves	4 cups
2	sweet onions, thinly sliced and separated into rings	1
6 Tbsp.	lemon-pepper liquid meat marinade	3 Tbsp.
2 oz.	thinly sliced dry-cured capocolla, crisp-cooked and drained	1 oz.
12	tomato slices	6

Pizza-Stuffed Burgers

Combine America's two favorite foods—burgers and pizza—and you're sure to make a lot of hungry people happy. Gently mix the ground beef and Italian sausage—overworking the mixture may make it tough.

PREP: 30 minutes
GRILL: 30 minutes

8 servings	ingredients	4 servings
3 lb.	ground beef sirloin	1½ lb.
8 oz.	bulk Italian sausage	4 oz.
2 tsp.	dried oregano, crushed	1 tsp.
½ tsp.	salt	¼ tsp.
½ tsp.	black pepper	¼ tsp.
8 thin slices	mozzarella cheese	4 thin slices
32 thin slices	pepperoni	16 thin slices
16 thin slices	hard salami	8 thin slices
16	fresh basil leaves	8
1 cup	sliced pitted ripe olives	½ cup
¼ tsp.	crushed red pepper (optional)	⅛ tsp.
2 cups	fresh baby spinach leaves	1 cup
8	ciabatta rolls, split and toasted	4
¼ cup	purchased marinara sauce, warmed	¼ cup
2 Tbsp.	Parmesan cheese curls (optional)	1 Tbsp.

1. In a large bowl combine ground beef, sausage, oregano, salt, and pepper. Mix lightly with clean hands.

2. Divide meat mixture into 16 portions. On a tray or baking sheet shape each portion into a 4½-inch-diameter patty. Divide mozzarella cheese, pepperoni, salami, basil, and olives among 8 of the patties. If desired, sprinkle with crushed red pepper. Top with the remaining 8 patties, pressing edges to seal well.

3. For a charcoal grill, arrange medium-hot coals around a drip pan. Check for medium heat above the pan. Place patties on grill rack over drip pan. Cover and grill about 30 minutes or until done (160°F). (For a gas grill, preheat grill. Reduce heat to medium. Adjust for indirect cooking. Place patties on grill rack over unlit burner. Grill as above.)

4. To assemble, place spinach leaves on bun bottoms. Add a patty to each bun bottom. Top patties with warmed marinara sauce and, if desired, Parmesan cheese. Add bun tops, cut sides down.

FOR 4 SERVINGS: Prepare using method above, except in Step 2 divide meat into eight portions. Divide mozzarella cheese, pepperoni, salami, basil, and olives among 4 of the patties. If desired, sprinkle with crushed red pepper. Top with the remaining 4 patties, pressing edges to seal well.

PER SERVING *791 cal., 48 g total fat (19 g sat. fat), 145 mg chol., 1,592 mg sodium, 32 g carbo., 2 g fiber, 57 g pro.*

Grilled Texas Steak Sandwiches

When a sandwich gets this good, it earns a ticket from the lunch table to the dinner table. To reduce the fat and calories a bit, substitute reduced-fat sour cream for the full-fat version.

1. Trim any fat from steaks; halve steaks crosswise. Lightly brush steaks with oil and sprinkle with salt and pepper. Grill directly over medium heat for 3 to 4 minutes per side or until desired doneness.

2. Meanwhile, for horseradish sauce, in a small bowl combine the sour cream, horseradish mustard, and dill; set aside.

3. Remove steaks to platter. Lightly brush each side of the bread with olive oil. Grill bread 1 minute per side. Serve steaks on grilled toast with horseradish sauce. Top with dill and additional salt and pepper.

PER SERVING *434 cal., 25 g total fat (8 g sat. fat), 71 mg chol., 485 mg sodium, 21 g carbo., 1 g fiber, 33 g pro.*

START TO FINISH: **20 minutes**

8 servings	ingredients	4 servings
4 10-oz.	top round steaks	2 10-oz.
	Olive oil	
	Salt and freshly ground black pepper	
½ cup	sour cream	¼ cup
4 to 6 Tbsp.	horseradish mustard	2 to 3 Tbsp.
2 Tbsp.	snipped fresh dill	1 Tbsp.
8	thick slices bread (for Texas toast)	4
	Fresh dill sprigs	

Corned Beef and Cabbage Calzone

Remember this recipe when you need an ingenious way to use St. Patrick's Day leftovers! Refrigerated pizza dough makes it simple to construct these savory half-moon pies.

1. Preheat oven to 400°F. Lightly grease 4 baking sheets; set aside.

2. In a large skillet cook caraway seeds over medium-high heat until lightly toasted. Add corned beef and red onion. Cook and stir for 2 minutes. Add slaw mixture and pepper. Cook 5 to 7 minutes or until wilted. Remove from heat; cover. Set aside. Drain before using if necessary.

3. On a lightly floured surface unroll pizza dough. Roll each dough into a 16×16-inch rectangle. Cut into quarters with a pizza cutter or kitchen shears. Place one-fourth of the mixture on each dough piece. Moisten edges with water and fold dough over filling to form a rectangle pocket. Roll edges up. Press edges with a fork to seal. Place on the prepared baking sheets.

4. Bake for 12 to 14 minutes until golden brown, rotating sheets halfway through baking time. Remove cooked pockets to a cooling rack using a large spatula. Cool 1 minute before serving.

5. If desired, serve with Thousand Island dressing.

FOR 4 SERVINGS: Prepare using method above, except in Step 1 grease 2 baking sheets. In Step 2 roll dough into one 16×16-inch rectangle.

PER SERVING *380 cal., 11 g total fat (3 g sat. fat), 42 mg chol., 1,206 mg sodium, 54 g carbo., 4 g fiber, 17 g pro.*

PREP: 8 minutes   COOK: 10 minutes
BAKE: 12 minutes   OVEN: 400°F

8 servings	ingredients	4 servings
2 tsp.	caraway seeds, lightly crushed	1 tsp.
12 oz.	cooked corned beef, finely chopped	6 oz.
1	red onion, thinly sliced	½
2 14- to 16-oz. pkg.	shredded cabbage with carrot (coleslaw mix)	1 14- to 16-oz. pkg.
1 tsp.	black pepper	½ tsp.
2 13.8-oz. pkg.	refrigerated pizza dough	1 13.8-oz. pkg.
	Bottled Thousand Island salad dressing (optional)	

Beefy Pasta Salad

When summer heat puts meal making into the "Do I have to?" category, go easy on yourself with main-dish salads such as this one. You may use deli roast beef—just ask the deli clerk to cut sandwich-style roast beef into ¼-inch-thick slices.

1. In a 6- to 8-quart Dutch oven cook pasta according to package directions, adding corn for the last 3 minutes of cooking time. Using tongs, transfer corn to a large cutting board. Drain pasta. Rinse in cold water and drain again; set aside. Cool corn until easy to handle.

2. Meanwhile, coat an unheated large nonstick skillet with cooking spray. Preheat skillet over medium-high heat. Add beef strips. Cook for 4 to 6 minutes or until slightly pink in the center, stirring occasionally. Remove from heat and cool slightly.

3. On a cutting board, place an ear of corn, pointed end down. Holding corn firmly at stem end to keep in place, use a sharp knife to cut corn from cob in planks; rotate cob to cut corn from all sides. Repeat with remaining ears of corn. In a large bowl combine pasta, beef, tomatoes, basil, and the ¼ cup Parmesan cheese.

4. In a screw-top jar combine vinegar, oil, garlic, salt, and pepper. Cover and shake well. Pour over pasta mixture; toss gently to coat. Gently fold in corn planks or place corn planks on top of individual servings. Serve immediately. If desired, garnish with additional Parmesan cheese.

FOR 4 SERVINGS: Prepare using method above, except in Step 1 use a 4- to 6-quart Dutch oven. In Step 3, use 2 tablespoons cheese.

PER SERVING *322 cal., 12 g total fat (3 g sat. fat), 38 mg chol., 256 mg sodium, 27 g carbo., 4 g fiber, 26 g pro.*

START TO FINISH: **30 minutes**

8 servings	ingredients	4 servings
2 cups	dried multigrain penne pasta	1 cup
4	ears corn, husks and silks removed	2
	Nonstick cooking spray	
24 oz.	boneless beef sirloin steak, cut into thin bite-size strips	12 oz.
2 cups	cherry tomatoes, halved	1 cup
½ cup	shredded fresh basil	¼ cup
¼ cup	finely shredded Parmesan cheese	2 Tbsp.
6 Tbsp.	white wine vinegar	3 Tbsp.
¼ cup	olive oil	2 Tbsp.
2 cloves	garlic, minced	1 clove
½ tsp.	salt	¼ tsp.
¼ tsp.	black pepper	⅛ tsp.
	Finely shredded Parmesan cheese (optional)	

Taco Salad

Check out this quick, easy, and absolutely failproof technique for making tortilla bowls at home. Once you have it down, you'll be making this tasty salad often.

1. For tortilla bowls, wrap tortillas in foil. Warm in a 350°F oven for 10 minutes. Coat eight 10-ounce custard cups with nonstick cooking spray. Carefully press 1 tortilla into each cup. Bake in the 350°F oven for 10 to 15 minutes or until golden and crisp. Cool; remove from custard cups.

2. Meanwhile, in a large skillet cook beef, onion, and garlic until beef is browned and onion is tender. Drain off fat.

3. Stir tomato sauce, vinegar, cumin, and crushed red pepper into skillet. Bring to boiling; reduce heat. Simmer, uncovered, for 10 minutes.

4. Place tortillas on 8 serving plates. Line tortillas with lettuce. Spoon beef mixture into tortillas. Sprinkle with cheese, sweet pepper (if desired), and tomatoes.

FOR 4 SERVINGS: Prepare using method above, except in Step 1 use four 10-ounce custard cups. In Step 4 place tortillas on 4 serving plates.

PER SERVING 297 cal., 13 g total fat (4 g sat. fat), 59 mg chol., 575 mg sodium, 23 g carbo., 3 g fiber, 22 g pro.

PREP: 35 minutes
BAKE: 20 minutes
OVEN: 350°F

8 servings	ingredients	4 servings
8 6- to 8-inch	whole wheat or plain flour tortillas	4 6- to 8-inch
	Nonstick cooking spray	
24 oz.	lean ground beef or uncooked ground turkey	12 oz.
1 cup	chopped onion	½ cup
2 cloves	garlic, minced	1 clove
2 8-oz. cans	tomato sauce	1 8-oz. can
2 Tbsp.	cider vinegar	1 Tbsp.
1 tsp.	ground cumin	½ tsp.
½ tsp.	crushed red pepper	¼ tsp.
8 cups	shredded lettuce	4 cups
½ cup	shredded reduced-fat cheddar cheese	¼ cup
½ cup	chopped green or red sweet pepper (optional)	¼ cup
24	cherry tomatoes, quartered	12

Italian Pork Chops on a Stick

Tote these marinated chops to your next tailgating event—you'll definitely rock the lot. With an entrée this sensational, side dishes can be as simple as a pasta salad, some marinated veggies, and a loaf of garlic bread.

1. For marinade, in a small bowl combine oil, vinegar, snipped rosemary, oregano, garlic, fennel seeds, basil, dry mustard, salt, and pepper.

2. Butterfly each pork chop by cutting horizontally to, but not through, the other side. Lay open the chops. Brush both sides of each chop with marinade. Place chops in a resealable plastic bag set in a shallow dish. Seal bag. Marinate in the refrigerator for 4 to 24 hours.

3. Remove chops from bag; discard marinade. Thread chops, accordion-style, onto eight 10- to 12-inch wooden or metal skewers, leaving enough room to hold one end of each skewer. (For additional stability, thread each chop onto two skewers.)

4. For a charcoal grill, grill chops on the rack of an uncovered grill directly over medium coals for 7 to 9 minutes or until chops are slightly pink in the center, turning once. If desired, for extra rosemary aroma add rosemary sprigs to the grill for the last 2 minutes of grilling. (For a gas grill, preheat grill. Reduce heat to medium. Place chops on grill rack over heat. Cover and grill as above.)

FOR 4 SERVINGS: Prepare using method above, except in Step 3 use four skewers.

PER SERVING *288 cal., 17 g total fat (4 g sat. fat), 95 mg chol., 360 mg sodium, 1 g carbo., 0 g fiber, 31 g pro.*

PREP: 20 minutes
MARINATE: 4 hours
GRILL: 7 minutes

8 servings	ingredients	4 servings
4 Tbsp.	olive oil	2 Tbsp.
2 Tbsp.	red wine vinegar	1 Tbsp.
4 tsp.	snipped fresh rosemary	2 tsp.
4 tsp.	snipped fresh oregano	2 tsp.
6 cloves	garlic, minced	3 cloves
2 tsp.	fennel seeds, crushed	1 tsp.
2 tsp.	dried basil, crushed	1 tsp.
1 tsp.	dry mustard	½ tsp.
1 tsp.	salt	½ tsp.
½ tsp.	black pepper	¼ tsp
8 5- to 6-oz.	boneless pork top loin chops, cut ¾ inch thick	4 5- to 6-oz.
	Fresh rosemary sprigs (optional)	

Chili-Peanut Pork Chops with Carrot-Cucumber Salad

In Asian cuisines, cucumbers are commonly used as a cooling counterpoint to other typically spicy ingredients. Nearly seedless English—sometimes called "hot house" or "burpless" cucumbers—usually come tightly wrapped in plastic.

START TO FINISH: **20 minutes**

8 servings	ingredients	4 servings
2 cups	dry-roasted peanuts	1 cup
4 tsp.	chili powder	2 tsp.
8	pork chops, cut ½ inch thick	4
¼ cup	olive oil	2 Tbsp.
½ cup	vinegar	¼ cup
2 Tbsp.	sugar	1 Tbsp.
6 small	carrots	3 small
2 small	English (seedless) cucumber	1 small
1 cup	fresh cilantro leaves	½ cup

1. Chop 1½ cups of the peanuts. In a shallow dish combine chopped peanuts and chili powder. Press both sides of pork chops into nut mixture to coat.

2. In a very large skillet heat olive oil over medium-high heat. Add chops; reduce heat to medium. Cook about 10 minutes or until done (160°F), turning once.

3. Meanwhile, for carrot-cucumber salad, in a medium bowl combine vinegar and sugar; stir until sugar is dissolved. Using a vegetable peeler, cut carrots and cucumber in ribbons. Add ribbons to vinegar mixture in bowl. Stir in remaining peanuts and the cilantro leaves.

4. Serve pork chops with carrot-cucumber salad. If desired, sprinkle with additional chili powder.

FOR 4 SERVINGS: Prepare using method above, except in Step 1 chop ¾ cup of the peanuts. In Step 2 use a large skillet.

PER SERVING *444 cal., 32 g total fat (6 g sat. fat), 52 mg chol., 97 mg sodium, 17 g carbo., 5 g fiber, 25 g pro.*

Garlic Pork and Sweet Potato Hash

This 30-minute supper is a supersimple twist on old-fashioned red flannel—or corned beef—hash. Pork tenderloins average 1½ pounds in weight. Buy two if you're serving eight.

1. In a microwave-safe bowl cook potatoes, covered with vented plastic wrap, for 8 minutes on high. Carefully uncover; stir once. Set aside. Meanwhile, to butterfly pork slices, cut three-quarters through each; open and flatten slightly. Brush with some of the soy sauce and lightly sprinkle with pepper.

2. In a large cook garlic in hot oil over medium-high heat just until it begins to turn golden. Remove garlic and set aside. Cook pork in the same skillet for 2 to 3 minutes per side until 145°F when tested with an instant-read thermometer. Transfer pork to a platter; cover. Add partially cooked potatoes to the skillet. Cook, stirring occasionally, until beginning to crisp. Add onions, cook for 1 minute. Spoon onto plates; top with pork and garlic.

3. For sauce, in the hot skillet whisk together honey, the water, and remaining soy sauce until bubbly. Drizzle sauce over pork.

PER SERVING *451 cal., 16 g total fat (3 g sat. fat), 107 mg chol., 449 mg sodium, 39 g carbo., 4 g fiber, 37 g pro.*

START TO FINISH: **30 minutes**

8 servings	ingredients	4 servings
6 small (8 cups)	sweet potatoes, scrubbed and chopped	3 small (4 cups)
3 lb.	pork tenderloin (cut into 1-inch slices)	1½ lb.
¼ cup	reduced-sodium soy sauce	2 Tbsp.
	Black pepper	
16 cloves	garlic, peeled and thinly sliced	8 cloves
6 Tbsp.	cooking oil	3 Tbsp.
4	green onions, sliced	2
¼ cup	honey	2 Tbsp.
2 Tbsp.	water	1 Tbsp.

Pork Loin with Butternut Squash

Imagine coming home to the aroma of this savory supper after work! To make butternut squash easier to peel, pierce it in several places with the tip of a paring knife, then microwave for 60 seconds before removing skin with a vegetable peeler.

1. Halve and peel squash, discard seeds, then cut squash into large chunks. Place squash in a 5- to 6-quart slow cooker.

2. In a small bowl combine salt, pepper, pumpkin pie spice, and onion or garlic powder; rub seasoning on all sides of pork. Heat oil in a large skillet; brown pork on all sides in the hot oil. Place pork on squash in cooker. Pour soup and applesauce over all. Cover and cook on low-heat setting for 4 hours or on high-heat setting for 2 hours.

3. Remove roast from cooker to cutting board to slice. Serve pork roast and squash drizzled with cooking sauce.

FOR 4 SERVINGS: Prepare using method above, except in Step 1 use a 3- or 3½-quart slow cooker.

PER SERVING *322 cal., 14 g total fat (4 g sat. fat), 76 mg chol., 732 mg sodium, 22 g carbo., 3 g fiber, 26 g pro.*

PREP: 20 minutes
SLOW COOK: 4 hours (low) or 2 hours (high)

8 servings	ingredients	4 servings
2 small	butternut squash	1 small
1 tsp.	each salt, black pepper, pumpkin pie spice, and onion or garlic powder	½ tsp.
2 to 3 lbs.	boneless pork loin roast	1 to 1½ lbs.
2 Tbsp.	olive oil	1 Tbsp.
2 18.8-oz. cans	caramelized French onion soup	1 18.8-oz. can
1 cup	chunky-style applesauce	½ cup

Sautéed Pork Chops with Apples

Granny Smith apples—perfectly balanced between sweet and tart—are an ideal accompaniment to pork, especially when the chops are rubbed with Sugar and Spice Rub. Leftover rub is excellent on ribs and pork burgers as well.

PREP: 20 minutes
CHILL: 1 hour
COOK: 18 minutes

8 servings	ingredients	4 servings
8 8-oz.	bone-in pork center-cut chops, cut ¾ inch thick	4 8-oz.
4 tsp.	canola oil	2 tsp.
2 Tbsp.	Sugar and Spice Rub	1 Tbsp.
2 Tbsp.	canola oil	1 Tbsp.
½ cup	dry white wine	¼ cup
4 cups	thinly sliced Granny Smith apples	2 cups
1 cup	reduced-sodium chicken broth or chicken stock	½ cup
2	fresh thyme sprigs	1
	Fresh thyme leaves	

1. Trim fat from chops. Brush the 4 teaspoons oil over all sides of chops. Sprinkle chops evenly with some of the Sugar and Spice Rub; rub in with your fingers. Cover with plastic wrap; chill in refrigerator for 1 hour.

2. Preheat a large skillet over medium-high heat for 2 minutes. Add the 2 tablespoons oil; swirl to lightly coat skillet. Add chops; cook for 10 to 12 minutes or until golden brown and juices run clear (145°F), turning once. Transfer chops to a warm platter; cover.

3. Remove skillet from heat. Slowly add wine to hot skillet, stirring to scrape up any browned bits from bottom of skillet. Return skillet to heat. Add sliced apples, broth, and thyme sprigs. Bring to boiling; reduce heat. Simmer, covered, about 3 minutes or just until apples are tender. Using a slotted spoon, transfer apples to a small bowl; cover and keep warm. Bring broth mixture in skillet to boiling. Boil about 5 minutes or until liquid is reduced by half. Return chops and apples to skillet; heat through. Garnish with fresh thyme leaves and serve immediately.

SUGAR AND SPICE RUB: In a small bowl stir together 2 tablespoons packed brown sugar, 2 teaspoons chili powder, 1½ teaspoons kosher salt, 1½ teaspoons garlic powder, 1½ teaspoons onion powder, 1½ teaspoons ground cumin, ¾ teaspoon cayenne pepper, and ¾ teaspoon black pepper. Store in an airtight container for up to 3 months. Makes about ½ cup.

FOR 4 SERVINGS: Prepare using method above, except in Step 1 use 2 teaspoons oil. In Step 2 use 1 tablespoon oil.

PER SERVING *297 cal., 12 g total fat (2 g sat. fat), 108 mg chol., 256 mg sodium, 9 g carbo., 2 g fiber, 35 g pro.*

Mushroom-Sauced Pork Chops

To clean fresh mushrooms before slicing, simply wipe debris away with a damp paper towel. Avoid washing mushrooms in water—if left too long in liquid, the spongy fungi will absorb the water, making their flavor less potent.

1. Trim fat from chops. In a large skillet heat oil over medium heat. Add chops; cook until browned, turning to brown evenly. Drain off fat. Coat the inside of a 5- or 6-quart slow cooker with cooking spray. Place onion in slow cooker. Add chops. Using a mortar and pestle, crush tapioca. In a medium bowl combine tapioca, mushroom soup, apple juice, Worcestershire sauce, thyme, and garlic powder; stir in mushrooms. Pour over chops in slow cooker.

2. Cover and cook on low-heat setting for 8 to 9 hours or on high-heat setting for 4 to 4½ hours. If desired, garnish with thyme sprigs.

FOR 4 SERVINGS: Prepare using method above, except in Step 1 use a 3½- or 4-quart slow cooker.

PER SERVING *330 cal., 10 g total fat (3 g sat. fat), 110 mg chol., 381 mg sodium, 17 g carbo., 1 g fiber, 39 g pro.*

PREP: 20 minutes
SLOW COOK: 8 hours (low) or 4 hours (high)

8 servings	ingredients	4 servings
8	pork loin chops, cut ¾ inch thick	4
2 Tbsp.	vegetable oil	1 Tbsp.
	Nonstick cooking spray	
2	onions, thinly sliced	1
¼ cup	quick-cooking tapioca	2 Tbsp.
2 10¾-oz. cans	reduced-fat and reduced-sodium condensed cream of mushroom soup	1 10¾-oz. can
1 cup	apple juice or apple cider	½ cup
2 tsp.	Worcestershire sauce	1 tsp.
4 tsp.	snipped fresh thyme or ¾ tsp. dried thyme, crushed	2 tsp.
½ tsp.	garlic powder	¼ tsp.
3 cups	sliced fresh mushrooms	1½ cups
	Fresh thyme sprigs (optional)	

Pork and Yellow Rice with Vegetables

New Orleans-style yellow rice gives this 30-minute dish pretty color and a good dose of traditional Cajun flair. To make sure the cauliflower florets cook evenly, cut them so that the head of each floret is about the size of a quarter.

1. In a large skillet heat oil over medium-high heat. Add pork and cumin seeds. Cook and stir for 2 minutes. Add onion and garlic; cook and stir for 2 minutes more. Drain off fat.

2. Cut any large carrots in half lengthwise. Add carrots, cauliflower, broth, water, and turmeric to skillet. Stir in uncooked rice. Bring to boiling; reduce heat. Simmer, covered, about 15 minutes or until rice is tender. Stir mixture gently. Sprinkle with green onions.

PER SERVING *403 cal., 12 g total fat (3 g sat. fat), 50 mg chol., 387 mg sodium, 46 g carbo., 2 g fiber, 25 g pro.*

START TO FINISH: **30 minutes**

10 servings	ingredients	5 servings
¼ cup	olive oil or vegetable oil	2 Tbsp.
2 lb.	lean boneless pork, cut into 1-inch pieces	1 lb.
1½ tsp.	cumin seeds, crushed	¾ tsp.
2	onions, halved and sliced	1
4 cloves	garlic, minced	2 cloves
2 cups	peeled baby baby carrots	1 cup
3 cups	cauliflower florets	1½ cups
2 14-oz. cans	chicken broth	1 14-oz. can
2 cups	water	1 cup
1 tsp.	ground turmeric	½ tsp.
2⅔ cups	uncooked long grain rice	1⅓ cups
½ cup	sliced green onions	¼ cup

Beer-Marinated Chops

If you've grown accustomed to the texture of pork being a bit on the dry side, you'll be glad to know that that the USDA reduced the safe internal temperature of pork from 160°F to 145°F so that pork retains its luscious juiciness.

PREP: 25 minutes
MARINATE: overnight
GRILL: 30 minutes

8 servings	ingredients	4 servings
8	bone-in pork rib or loin chops, cut 1½ inches thick	4
2 12-oz. bottles	honey-wheat beer	1 12-oz. bottle
2 Tbsp.	olive oil	1 Tbsp.
4 cloves	garlic, minced	2 cloves
1 tsp.	coarse-ground black pepper	½ tsp.
½ tsp.	salt	¼ tsp.
2 cups	shredded white cheddar cheese or crumbled blue cheese (optional)	1 cup
½ cup	thinly sliced green onions (optional)	¼ cup
4 Tbsp.	chopped walnuts, toasted* (optional)	2 Tbsp.
	Fresh herb sprigs (optional)	

1. Trim fat from chops. Place chops in a resealable plastic bag set in a shallow dish. For marinade, in a medium bowl combine beer, oil, garlic, ½ teaspoon of the pepper, and the salt. Pour marinade over chops; seal bag. Marinate in the refrigerator overnight, turning bag occasionally.

2. Drain chops, discarding marinade. For a charcoal grill, arrange medium-hot coals around a drip pan. Test for medium heat above pan. Place chops on grill rack over drip pan. Cover and grill for 30 to 35 minutes or until chops are slightly pink in center and juices run clear (145°F.) (For a gas grill, preheat grill. Reduce heat to medium. Adjust for indirect cooking. Grill as above.)

3. If desired, combine cheese, green onions, walnuts, and the remaining ½ teaspoon pepper. Carefully spoon cheese topping over chops. Cover and grill for 2 to 3 minutes more or until cheese is melted. If desired, garnish with fresh herb sprigs.

FOR 4 SERVINGS: Prepare using method above, except in Step 1 use ¼ teaspoon of the pepper and in Step 3 use the remaining ¼ teaspoon of the pepper.

PER SERVING *428 cal., 17 g total fat (8 g sat. fat), 160 mg chol., 595 mg sodium, 2 g carbo., 0 g fiber, 61 g pro.*

***NOTE:** To toast nuts, seeds, or shredded coconut, spread pieces in a single layer in a shallow baking pan. Bake in a 350°F oven for 5 to 10 minutes or until pieces are golden brown, stirring once or twice.

Green Chile Pork Stew

Dredging cubed pork in a mixture of ground cumin and flour not only infuses the pork with warm Mexican flavor, it thickens the liquids to form a smooth, gravylike sauce. Salsa verde may also be labeled "Green Chile Salsa."

1. In a large self-sealing plastic bag combine flour and ground cumin. Add pork, seal bag and toss to coat.

2. In a large skillet heat olive oil over medium heat. Add pork and any remaining flour mixture to skillet. Cook for 8 minutes, stirring occasionally, until pork is well browned. Remove pork from skillet. Stir in 1½ cups water, salsa verde, and corn, scraping up any browned bits. Bring to boiling. Add pork to skillet and heat through.

3. Ladle into bowls and top each serving with 1 tablespoon sour cream and, if desired, cilantro, lime wedges, and a sprinkle of ground cumin. If desired, serve with corn bread.

FOR 4 SERVINGS: Prepare using method above, except in Step 2 use ¾ cup water.

PER SERVING *375 cal., 22 g total fat (8 g sat. fat), 81 mg chol., 413 mg sodium, 15 g carbo., 1 g fiber, 28 g pro.*

START TO FINISH: **25 minutes**

8 servings	ingredients	4 servings
½ cup	all-purpose flour	¼ cup
2 tsp.	ground cumin	1 tsp.
2½ lb.	boneless pork loin, cut into ¾- to 1-inch pieces	1¼ lb.
2 tsp.	olive oil	2 tsp.
2 cups	mild salsa verde	1 cup
2 12-oz. pkg.	frozen corn with red and/or green peppers or frozen whole kernel corn	1 12-oz. pkg.
½ cup	sour cream	¼ cup
	Fresh cilantro, lime wedges, and ground cumin (optional)	
	Corn bread (optional)	

Apple Butter-Glazed Ham

For supersweet Brussels sprouts, select smaller heads. To trim them, simply cut away about ¼ inch of the stem end with a sharp paring knife and remove a few of the outermost leaves.

1. In a large covered saucepan cook sweet potatoes and Brussels sprouts in enough boiling, lightly salted water to cover for 8 or 10 minutes or just until tender; drain.

2. Meanwhile, in a very large skillet melt butter over medium-high heat. Add ham; cook for 4 to 5 minutes or until lightly browned, turning occasionally. Remove ham from skillet; cover to keep warm.

3. Add apple butter and vinegar to skillet; cook and stir until heated through. Serve ham and vegetables with apple butter mixture. Season with salt and pepper.

PER SERVING *513 cal., 16 g total fat (7 g sat. fat), 80 mg chol., 1,664 mg sodium, 71 g carbo., 8 g fiber, 23 g pro.*

START TO FINISH: **20 minutes**

8 servings	ingredients	4 servings
4 medium	sweet potatoes, peeled, halved lengthwise, and sliced ½ inch thick	2 medium
24 oz.	Brussels sprouts, trimmed and halved	12 oz.
¼ cup	butter	2 Tbsp.
2 to 2½ lb.	sliced cooked ham, about ¼ inch thick	1 to 1¼ lb.
1 cup	apple butter	½ cup
4 Tbsp.	cider vinegar	2 Tbsp.
	Salt and black pepper	

Ultimate Grilled Cheese and Ham Panini

To ripen fresh pears, place firm pears in a brown paper bag at room temperature. Check the pears daily by pressing gently at their stems. Once the pears yield to gentle pressure, their silky texture will be perfect for these sensational sandwiches.

PREP: 25 minutes
COOK: 6 minutes

8 servings	ingredients	4 servings
2 16-oz. loaves or 16 slices	unsliced ciabatta or Italian bread or sourdough or multigrain bread, sliced ½- to ¾-inch thick	1 16-oz. loaf or 8 slices
1 cup	chutney (any flavor)	½ cup
6 oz.	thinly sliced Fontina, Jarlsberg, Gruyère, or Swiss cheese	3 oz.
16 oz.	thinly sliced cooked ham	8 oz.
2	Bosc or Anjou pears or apples, cored and thinly sliced	1
2 cups	fresh baby arugula or spinach	1 cup
6 oz.	thinly sliced Gouda, Edam, Muenster, or provolone cheese	3 oz.
4 to 6 Tbsp.	butter, softened, or olive oil	2 to 3 Tbsp.

1. If using bread loaves, carefully trim off and discard the top crust of the bread to make a flat surface if necessary. Turn bread over; trim off and discard bottom crust, if necessary. Cut remaining bread loaf in half horizontally to form two ½-inch-thick slices.

2. Preheat an electric sandwich press, a covered indoor grill, a grill pan, or a very large skillet over medium-low heat for 1 to 2 minutes.

3. If needed, snip any large pieces of chutney. Spread chutney on one side of each slice of bread. Place the Fontina cheese on half the loaf or on 8 of the bread slices. Top with ham, pear, arugula, the Gouda cheese and the other half of bread loaf or remaining slices. Spread both sides of loaf or sandwiches evenly with butter or brush with oil. Cut loaf crosswise into four sandwiches.

4. Place sandwiches (two at a time if necessary) in the sandwich press or indoor grill. Cover and cook for 6 to 8 minutes or until bread is toasted and cheese melts. (If using a grill pan or skillet, place sandwiches in pan. Weight sandwiches down with a heavy skillet or a pie plate containing a can of vegetables. Cook until bread is lightly toasted. Using hot pads, carefully remove top skillet. Turn sandwiches over, weight down, and cook until bread is toasted and cheese melts.)

FOR 4 SERVINGS: Prepare using method above, except in Step 3 place Fontina cheese on half the loaf or 4 bread slices.

PER SERVING 659 cal., 25 g total fat (14 g sat. fat), 101 mg chol., 1,867 mg sodium, 78 g carbo., 4 g fiber, 30 g pro.

Hot Ham and Pear Melts

Nestled in hollowed French baguettes, savory ham, arugula, and goat cheese join sweet-tart apricot preserves and tender, juicy pears to create the kind of crispy, oven-baked sandwich that memories are made of.

1. Preheat oven to 350°F. Cut each baguette crosswise into four portions. Split each portion in half horizontally. Scoop out the soft centers of tops and bottoms of baguette portions, leaving about a ½-inch shell. (Save soft bread centers for another use.)

2. Spread preserves on cut sides of bottom halves of baguette portions. Top with ham, pear slices, and arugula. In a small bowl stir together goat cheese and chives; spread on cut sides of the top halves of the baguette portions. Place on arugula, cheese sides down. Lightly coat tops and bottoms of sandwiches with cooking spray.

3. Place sandwiches in a shallow baking pan. Cover with foil. Bake for 10 to 15 minutes or until heated through. Serve warm.

PER SERVING *300 cal., 10 g total fat (5 g sat. fat), 32 mg chol., 647 mg sodium, 36 g carbo., 3 g fiber, 16 g pro.*

PREP: **15 minutes**
BAKE: **10 minutes**
OVEN: **350°F**

8 servings	ingredients	4 servings
2 10- to 12-oz.	whole grain baguette	1 10- to 12 oz.
4 Tbsp.	lower-sugar apricot preserves	2 Tbsp.
12 oz.	thinly sliced lower-sodium cooked ham	6 oz.
2 medium	pears, quartered, cored, and thinly sliced	1 medium
4 cups	arugula or fresh spinach	2 cups
2 4-oz. pkg.	goat cheese (chèvre), softened	1 4-oz. pkg.
2 tsp.	snipped fresh chives	1 tsp.
	Nonstick cooking spray	

Sausage and Bean Jambalaya

If you can, do try to locate true andouille—the traditional spicy, heavily smoked pork sausage—for this jazzy jambalaya. When slow-cooked, andouille will imbue the dish with classic Louisiana flavor.

1. Slice sausage into 1-inch chunks. Stem, seed, and coarsely chop sweet peppers.

2. In a 5- to 6-quart slow cooker combine the sausage, sweet peppers, drained beans, undrained tomatoes, and celery. Cover and cook on low-heat setting for 4 hours high-heat setting for 2 hours.

FOR 4 SERVINGS: Prepare using method above, except in Step 2 use a 3½- or 4-quart slow cooker.

PER SERVING *409 cal., 24 g total fat (8 g sat. fat), 56 mg chol., 1,295 mg sodium, 32 g carbo., 8 g fiber, 18 g pro.*

PREP: 15 minutes
SLOW COOK: 4 hours (low) or 2 hours (high)

8 servings	ingredients	4 servings
24 oz.	cooked andouille sausage or cooked kielbasa (Polska kielbasa)	12 oz.
4	large yellow and/or orange sweet peppers	2
2 15- to 16-oz. cans	red kidney beans, rinsed and drained	1 15- to 16-oz. can
2 14.5-oz. cans	fire-roasted diced tomatoes	1 14.5-oz. can
2 cups	chopped celery	1 cup

CHAPTER 4

Seafood

Whenever you think there's nothing new to serve for supper, consider seafood. Versatile fish and shellfish lend themselves to a whole variety of lickety-split cooking methods. Fish a fabulous find for midweek meals as well company-special dinners.

120

125

129

Lemon and Herb Grilled Trout Sandwiches

Quick-cooking trout remains perfectly tender thanks to a coat of herbed mayonnaise. When selecting trout, choose fillets that glisten, look flawless, and smell clean and fresh. The flesh should be firm and spring back when pressed.

1. Finely shred peel and squeeze juice from 1 lemon; thinly slice the remaining lemon and set aside. In a small bowl combine mayonnaise, lemon peel, lemon juice, basil, salt, and pepper.

2. Rinse fish; pat dry. Remove ¼ cup of the mayonnaise mixture and brush onto fish. Place fish, skin sides up, on the rack of an uncovered grill directly over medium-high heat; grill for 1 minute. Carefully turn skin sides down and grill 5 to 7 minutes more or just until fish flakes easily with a fork. Add lemon slices and halved buns, cut sides down, to the grill after turning fish.

3. Remove fish, buns, and lemon slices from grill. If desired, remove skin from fish. Cut fish into bun-size pieces. Top bun bottoms with some of the mayonnaise mixture. Add fish, lemon slices, and, if desired, additional basil. Pass any remaining mayonnaise mixture.

FOR 4 SERVINGS: Prepare using method above, except in Step 1 finely shred peel from lemon; juice half the lemon; thinly slice remaining lemon half and set aside. In Step 2 remove 2 tablespoons of the mayonnaise mixture and brush onto fish.

PER SERVING 518 cal., 30 g total fat (6 g sat. fat), 77 mg chol., 667 mg sodium, 32 g carbo., 3 g fiber, 29 g pro.

START TO FINISH: **22 minutes**

8 servings	ingredients	4 servings
2	large lemons	1
1 cup	mayonnaise	½ cup
½ cup	snipped fresh basil	¼ cup
½ tsp.	salt	¼ tsp.
½ tsp.	black pepper	¼ tsp.
2 lb.	ruby or rainbow trout fillets	1 lb.
8	ciabatta buns, split	4
	Fresh basil (optional)	

Crisp Catfish with Apple-Celery Slaw

START TO FINISH: 25 minutes

8 servings	ingredients	4 servings
2	lemon	1
⅔ cup	mayonnaise	⅓ cup
2 Tbsp.	honey	1 Tbsp.
6	stalks celery, thinly sliced	3
2	Granny Smith apple, thinly sliced	1
2 cups	shredded red cabbage	1 cup
2 to 3 lb.	catfish fillets	1 to 1½ lb.
⅔ cup	yellow cornmeal	⅓ cup
2 tsp.	chili powder	1 tsp.
	Canola oil	

This is a meal you can feel good about—American farm-raised catfish is one of the most sustainable fish you can buy. And with the colorful, fiber-filled slaw, dinner becomes both nutritious and delicious.

1. Cut 1 lemon into slices or wedges; set aside. Juice remaining lemon into a large bowl. For slaw, combine mayonnaise and honey with juice; reserve 4 tablespoons juice mixture. Stir celery, apple, and cabbage into juice mixture in bowl; set aside.

2. Sprinkle catfish fillets with 1 teaspoon salt and brush with reserved juice mixture. In shallow dish combine cornmeal and chili powder; coat fish with mixture.

3. In a large skillet heat 4 tablespoons oil over medium heat. Cook fish in hot oil 3 to 4 minutes per side until golden and fish flakes easily with a fork. Serve fish with slaw and lemon.

FOR 4 SERVINGS: Prepare using method above, except in Step 1 cut half of 1 lemon into slices or wedges and juice remaining half into a large bowl. Reserve 2 tablespoons juice mixture. In Step 2 sprinkle catfish with ½ teaspoon salt. In Step 3 heat 2 tablespoons oil over medium heat.

PER SERVING 446 cal., 31 g total fat (5 g sat. fat), 60 mg chol., 488 mg sodium, 25 g carbo., 4 g fiber, 19 g pro.

Fish and Chips-Style Cod

In this low-calorie batter, beer acts as a leavening that makes the batter fry up light, crisp, and crunchy. Make "chips" to accompany the fish by baking frozen french fries—look for the words "extra-crispy" on the label—serve chips that taste almost like the real thing.

PREP: 20 minutes   CHILL: 30 minutes
COOK: 4 minutes per batch
OVEN: 250°F

8 servings	ingredients	4 servings
2 lb.	fresh or frozen cod or halibut fillets	1 lb.
1 cup	flour	½ cup
⅔ cup	fat-free milk	⅓ cup
⅔ cup	ale or nonalcoholic beer	⅓ cup
2	eggs	1
½ tsp.	kosher salt	¼ tsp.
	freshly ground black pepper	
1 cup	canola oil	½ cup
	Malt vinegar	

1. Thaw fish, if frozen. Set aside. In a medium bowl whisk together flour, milk, ale, egg, salt, and pepper until combined. Cover and chill batter for 30 minutes.

2. Preheat oven to 250°F. Rinse fish under cold running water; pat dry with paper towels. Cut fish crosswise into eight pieces total.

3. In a large skillet heat oil over medium-high heat for 2 minutes. Dip four pieces of the fish in the batter, turning to coat and letting excess batter drip off. Fry the fish pieces in the hot oil about 4 minutes or until golden brown and fish flakes easily when tested with a fork, turning once. Transfer fried fish to paper towels; let stand to drain. Place fish on a baking sheet; keep warm in the oven. Repeat with remaining fish pieces.

4. Serve fish with malt vinegar.

FOR 4 SERVINGS: Prepare using method above, except in Step 2 cut fish into four pieces total.

PER SERVING *177 cal., 8 g total fat (1 g sat. fat), 55 mg chol., 118 mg sodium, 4 g carbo., 0 g fiber, 21 g pro.*

Barbecued Salmon with Corn Relish

Three great foods—salmon, sweet corn, and barbecue sauce—make a tasty trio in this grilled supper. If you can, opt for wild salmon—it's more flavorful and contains more heart-healthy omega 3 fatty acids than the farmed salmon.

1. Thinly slice 1 jalapeño; seed and finely chop remaining pepper. In a medium bowl combine chopped jalapeño and sweet pepper; set aside.

2. Place corn on the rack of an uncovered grill directly over medium heat. Grill, turning occasionally, for 10 to 15 minutes or until crisp-tender. Transfer corn to a cutting board; cool slightly.

3. Meanwhile, rinse salmon and pat dry; sprinkle with salt and black pepper. Add to grill. Grill 4 to 6 minutes or until fish flakes easily when tested with a fork, turning once. Cover salmon to keep warm. Cut corn from cob. Add to chopped peppers with 2 tablespoons of the barbecue sauce, the oil, ½ teaspoon salt, and ½ teaspoon black pepper.

4. Serve salmon with corn relish. Top with remaining barbecue sauce and, if desired, fresh herb.

FOR 4 SERVINGS: Prepare using method above, except in Step 1 slice half of the jalapeño and seed and chop the remaining half. In Step 3 cut corn from cob. Add to chopped peppers with 1 tablespoon of the barbecue sauce, the oil, ¼ teaspoon salt, and ¼ teaspoon black pepper.

PER SERVING *395 cal., 22 g total fat (5 g sat. fat), 78 mg chol., 470 mg sodium, 18 g carbo., 2 g fiber, 31 g pro.*

START TO FINISH: **30 minutes**

8 servings	ingredients	4 servings
2	jalapeños (see note, page 54)	1
2	red sweet peppers, chopped	1
4	ears fresh sweet corn, husked	2
8 5- to 6-oz.	skinless salmon fillets, ½ to 1 inch thick	4 5- to 6-oz.
	Salt	
	Black pepper	
1 cup	bottled barbecue sauce	½ cup
4 tsp.	olive oil	2 tsp.
½ tsp.	salt	¼ tsp.
½ tsp.	black pepper	¼ tsp.
	Fresh marjoram or oregano (optional)	

Double-Play Salmon Burgers

Grinding a small amount of smoked salmon along with the fresh salmon is pure genius—the smoked salmon lends luxurious texture as well as making the pan-fried patties taste as smoky as if they were grilled outdoors.

8 servings	ingredients	4 servings
10	ciabatta buns	5
24 oz.	skinless, boneless salmon fillets	12 oz.
6	green onions	3
2	eggs	1
2 tsp.	seafood seasoning	1 tsp.
6 oz.	smoked salmon, hot-style (skinned and boned) or lox	3 oz.
2 Tbsp.	olive oil	1 Tbsp.
⅔ cup	mayonnaise	⅓ cup
	Cucumber and green onions, diagonally sliced	

1. In a food processor process 2 buns to coarse crumbs. Transfer crumbs to large bowl.

2. Coarsely chop salmon fillets and green onions. In processor pulse to coarsely grind salmon and onions. Add the eggs, ½ teaspoon of the seafood seasoning, and two-thirds the smoked salmon. Pulse to combine. Transfer to bowl with crumbs. Mix, then shape into eight 3½-inch patties.

3. In large nonstick skillet heat oil over medium heat. Cook patties 5 to 6 minutes per side, just until golden and cooked through. Meanwhile, toast buns and finely chop remaining smoked salmon.

4. For sauce, combine chopped salmon, mayo, and remaining seafood seasoning. Spoon some sauce on bun bottoms. To each add a patty, then top with cucumber and onions. Pass remaining sauce.

FOR 4 SERVINGS: Prepare using method above, except in Step 1 process 1 bun. In Step 2 use 1 egg, ¼ teaspoon of the seafood seasoning, and two-thirds of the smoked salmon. Shape into four 3½-inch patties.

PER SERVING *659 cal., 33 g total fat (7 g sat. fat), 110 mg chol., 882 mg sodium, 59 g carbo., 2 g fiber, 34 g pro.*

Salmon Melts

The next time you have salmon for supper, consider cooking an extra fillet or two to save for these extraordinary open-face sandwiches. Another time, try topping the melts with shredded dilled Havarti cheese.

1. Preheat broiler. In a medium bowl stir together salmon, onions, sweet pepper, mayonnaise, sour cream, lemon juice, and hot pepper sauce. Arrange English muffin halves on a baking sheet. Top evenly with tomato slices, salmon mixture, and the cheese. Broil 4 to 5 inches from the heat for 3 to 4 minutes or until cheese melts and bubbles. Top with arugula.

PER SERVING *244 cal., 11 g total fat (3 g sat. fat), 48 mg chol., 348 mg sodium, 17 g carbo., 3 g fiber, 20 g pro.*

PREP: 20 minutes
BROIL: 3 minutes

8 servings	ingredients	4 servings
16 oz.	cooked salmon, flaked	8 oz.
½ cup	finely chopped green onions	¼ cup
½ cup	finely chopped red sweet pepper	¼ cup
¼ cup	fat-free mayonnaise dressing	2 Tbsp.
¼ cup	light sour cream	2 Tbsp.
4 tsp.	lemon juice	2 tsp.
½ tsp.	bottled hot pepper sauce	¼ tsp.
4	whole wheat English muffins, split and toasted	2
8 slices	tomato	4 slices
1 cup	shredded part-skim mozzarella cheese	½ cup
2 cups	arugula or watercress	1 cup

Dilled Tuna and Potato Salad

With the addition of a loaf of crusty bread, this substantial main-dish salad makes a filling lunch or supper. For the most fabulous flavor, mix the salad while the potatoes are still a bit warm so that they absorb the delicious dressing.

1. Scrub potatoes; cut into ½-inch pieces. In a large covered saucepan cook potatoes in enough boiling water to cover for 10 to 12 minutes or just until tender. Drain and cool slightly.

2. Meanwhile, in a large bowl stir together mayonnaise, yogurt, dill, milk, garlic, lemon peel, and salt. Stir in cucumber, green onions, and radishes. Add cooked potato, tuna, and hard-cooked eggs; toss gently to coat. Cover and chill for 4 to 6 hours.

3. To serve, line serving bowls with cabbage leaves. Gently stir tuna mixture; spoon onto cabbage. If desired, garnish with fresh dill sprigs and season with crackled black pepper.

PER SERVING *243 cal., 10 g total fat (2 g sat. fat), 96 mg chol., 461 mg sodium, 22 g carbo., 5 g fiber, 18 g pro.*

PREP: 25 minutes
CHILL: 4 hours

12 servings	ingredients	6 servings
6 (2 lb.)	red-skin potatoes	3 (1 lb.)
1 cup	light mayonnaise or salad dressing	½ cup
1 cup	plain fat-free yogurt	½ cup
2 Tbsp.	snipped fresh dill	1 Tbsp.
2 Tbsp.	fat-free milk	1 Tbsp.
2 cloves	garlic, minced	1 clove
1 tsp.	finely shredded lemon peel	½ tsp.
½ tsp.	salt	¼ tsp.
2 cups	chopped cucumber	1 cup
½ cup	sliced green onions	¼ cup
½ cup	coarsely chopped radishes	¼ cup
2 9.25-oz. cans	chunk white tuna (water pack), drained and broken into chunks	1 9.25-oz. can
4	hard-cooked eggs, chopped	2
4 cups	shredded savoy cabbage or napa cabbage leaves	2 cups
	Fresh dill sprigs (optional)	
	Cracked black pepper (optional)	

Asian-Style Tuna Kabobs

Rice vinegar—a staple in Asian cuisine—is mild, sweet, and less acidic than other vinegars. Should you need to substitute, use an equal amount of cider vinegar along with a ½ teaspoon sugar or honey.

PREP: 25 minutes
MARINATE: 45 minutes
GRILL: 6 minutes

8 servings	ingredients	4 servings
3 lb.	fresh or frozen tuna steaks	1½ lb.
⅔ cup	rice vinegar	⅓ cup
¼ cup	grated fresh ginger	½ cup
¼ cup	peanut oil	½ cup
¼ cup	toasted sesame oil	½ cup
¼ cup	soy sauce	½ cup
¼ cup	honey	½ cup
¼ cup	tahini (sesame seed paste) (optional)	2 Tbsp.
¼ cup	snipped fresh cilantro	2 Tbsp.
2	fresh serrano chile peppers, stemmed, seeded, and finely chopped (see note, page 54)	1
2	medium yellow sweet peppers, cut into 1-inch pieces	1
16	green onions, trimmed and each cut into 4 pieces	8
	Black sesame seeds and/or toasted regular sesame seeds (optional)	

1. Thaw fish, if frozen. Rinse fish; pat dry with paper towels. Cut fish into 1¼-inch cubes.

2. For marinade, in a medium bowl combine rice vinegar, ginger, peanut oil, sesame oil, soy sauce, honey, tahini (if desired), cilantro, and chile. Divide the mixture in half. Set aside half the marinade to use as a dipping sauce. Add fish cubes to remaining mixture; mix gently to coat. Cover and marinate in the refrigerator for 45 minutes (do not marinate any longer).

3. Drain fish, reserving marinade. On eight long skewers,* alternately thread fish cubes, sweet pepper pieces, and green onion pieces.

4. For a charcoal grill, grill kabobs on the rack of an uncovered grill directly over medium coals for 6 to 8 minutes or until fish is pink in the center but flakes easily when tested with a fork, turning once halfway through grilling and brushing frequently with the reserved marinade for the first 4 minutes of grilling. (For a gas grill, preheat grill. Reduce heat to medium. Place kabobs on grill rack over heat. Cover and grill as above.) Discard any remaining marinade. Serve immediately with the dipping sauce; if desired, sprinkle with sesame seeds.

FOR 4 SERVINGS: Prepare using method above, except in Step 3 use four long skewers.

PER SERVING *257 cal., 14 g total fat (3 g sat. fat), 32 mg chol., 418 mg sodium, 10 g carbo., 1 g fiber, 21 g pro.*

*****NOTE** If using wooden skewers, soak in water for 30 minutes before grilling.

Coconut-Poached Mahi Mahi

In Hawaiian, mahi mahi means "very strong"—a description that most certainly applies to the fish's strength as a swimmer and not to its flavor, which is exceptionally clean and mild. Be sure to shake canned coconut milk vigorously before using—its solids tend to fall to the bottom.

1. Finely shred peel from lime, then juice the lime. Set aside the peel. In a large saucepan over medium heat combine the lime juice, coconut milk, chile slices, and sugar.

2. Cut fish into 16 portions; rinse and pat dry with paper towels. Rub salt on fish portions, then place in coconut milk mixture in saucepan. Cook fish, covered, for 5 minutes. Uncover; gently stir in bok choy. Cook for 3 to 5 minutes more or until fish flakes easily when tested with a fork. Ladle fish with cooking liquid into bowls. Top with lime peel and, if desired, ginger and green chiles.

FOR 4 SERVINGS: Prepare using method above, except in Step 2 cut fish into 8 portions.

PER SERVING *189 cal., 7 g total fat (4 g sat. fat), 83 mg chol., 744 mg sodium, 10 g carbo., 1 g fiber, 22 g pro.*

START TO FINISH: 20 minutes

8 servings	ingredients	4 servings
2	limes	1
2 15-oz. cans	light coconut milk	1 15-oz. can
2	Thai green chiles, thinly sliced (see note, page 54)	1
2 Tbsp.	sugar	1 Tbsp.
2 lb.	skinless, boneless mahi mahi or other firm whitefish fillets	1 lb.
2 tsp.	salt	1 tsp.
6 cups	torn bok choy	3 cups
	Crystallized ginger, green chilies (optional)	

Cajun Snapper with Red Beans and Rice

If your fillets vary in thickness, they will cook evenly if you place the thicker part of the fillet toward the center of the pan—where it is hottest—and the thinner part of the fillet toward the edge of the pan, where it will cook more slowly.

1. In a medium saucepan cook frankfurters over medium heat for 2 to 3 minutes until heated through. Stir in rice, 1 cup water, 2 teaspoons of the Cajun seasoning, and the beans. Cook, covered, for 15 minutes over medium-low heat.

2. Meanwhile, rinse fish; pat dry with paper towels. In a very large skillet melt the butter over medium heat. In a shallow dish combine flour and remaining 4 teaspoons Cajun seasoning. Press top sides of fish into the flour mixture, then place fish, skin sides down, in hot butter. Cook for 3 to 5 minutes until skin is crisp. Carefully turn fish with a metal spatula. Cook for 3 to 5 minutes longer or until fish flakes easily with a fork.

3. Serve fish over rice and beans. Drizzle with pan juices and snip fresh parsley over the top.

FOR 4 SERVINGS: Prepare using method above, except in Step 1 use ½ cup water and 1 teaspoon of the Cajun seasoning. In Step 2 use a large skillet and remaining 2 teaspoons Cajun seasoning.

PER SERVING *438 cal., 16 g total fat (7 g sat. fat), 69 mg chol., 544 mg sodium, 41 g carbo., 6 g fiber, 36 g pro.*

START TO FINISH: **25 minutes**

8 servings	ingredients	4 servings
4	frankfurters, chopped	2
2 8.8-oz. pkg.	fully cooked rice	1 8.8-oz. pkg.
1 cup	water	½ cup
2 Tbsp.	salt-free Cajun seasoning	1 Tbsp.
2 15- to 16-oz. cans	red beans, rinsed and drained	1 15- to 16-oz. can
	Bottled hot pepper sauce (optional)	
2 lb.	pollock, striped bass, or red snapper fillets, cut into 4 pieces	1 lb.
¼ cup	butter	2 Tbsp.
¼ cup	all-purpose flour	2 Tbsp.
	Fresh parsley (optional)	

Fast Shrimp Bisque

Because shrimp shells are loaded with flavor, cooking the shell-on shrimp in water gets this soup's broth off to a delicious start. Anchovy paste comes in squeeze tubes and is shelved near the canned tuna in most grocery stores.

1. For broth, in a 6-quart Dutch oven combine the water, Old Bay Seasoning, shrimp, and celery. Cook, uncovered, over medium-high heat for 5 to 8 minutes or until shrimp shells turn pink and shrimp are opaque. Remove shrimp with slotted spoon or tongs; set aside to cool.

2. In a medium bowl whisk together evaporated milk, milk, flour, and anchovy paste; stir into broth in Dutch oven. Cook, uncovered, over medium heat for 10 minutes, stirring occasionally.

3. Meanwhile, peel shrimp. Chop about half the shrimp. Add chopped shrimp to soup. Cook for 1 to 2 minutes or until heated through. Ladle into bowls. Top with remaining shrimp. Pass additional seafood seasoning.

VARIATION: For a spicy curry seafood soup, use coconut milk in place of evaporated milk and add a little curry powder and Asian chili sauce.

FOR 4 SERVINGS: Prepare using method above, except in Step 1 use a 4-quart Dutch oven.

PER SERVING *224 cal., 9 g total fat (5 g sat. fat), 138 mg chol., 973 mg sodium, 16 g carbo., 0 g fiber, 20 g pro.*

START TO FINISH: **25 minutes**

8 servings	ingredients	4 servings
4 cups	water	2 cups
4 tsp.	Old Bay Seasoning or other seafood seasoning	2 tsp.
24 oz.	fresh or frozen medium shrimp in shells, thawed	12 oz.
2 cups (2 stalks)	celery, thinly sliced	1 cup (1 stalk)
1 12-oz. can	evaporated milk	½ 12-oz. can
2 cups	milk	1 cup
¼ cup	all-purpose flour	2 Tbsp.
4 tsp.	anchovy paste or 1 or 2 anchovies, finely chopped	2 tsp.
	Seafood seasoning (optional)	

Lemon-Dill Shrimp and Pasta

Leftover fresh dill will find a home in many dishes through the week. Clip ¼ inch from the bottoms of its stems and place upright in a glass with the stems immersed in ½ inch of water. Cover loosely with a plastic bag and refrigerate.

1. Rinse shrimp; pat dry with paper towels. Finely shred 2 teaspoons peel from the lemon; set aside peel. Juice the lemons over a bowl; set aside juice. Cook pasta according to package directions.

2. Meanwhile, in a large skillet heat olive oil over medium heat. Cook garlic in hot oil for 1 minute. Add shrimp; cook for 3 to 4 minutes, turning frequently, until shrimp are opaque. Add spinach and drained pasta; toss just until spinach begins to wilt. Stir in Italian seasoning, lemon peel, and 2 tablespoons of the lemon juice. Season to taste with salt and pepper. Top with fresh dill. Serve at once.

FOR 4 SERVINGS: Prepare using method above, except in Step 1 finely shred 1 teaspoon peel from the lemon; set aside peel. Juice the lemon.

PER SERVING *359 cal., 9 g total fat (1 g sat. fat), 107 mg chol., 696 mg sodium, 50 g carbo., 5 g fiber, 21 g pro.*

VARIATIONS: Substitute bite-size pieces of deli-roasted chicken for the shrimp. For a peppery bite, replace half the spinach with arugula.

START TO FINISH: **25 minutes**

8 servings	ingredients	4 servings
24 oz.	frozen peeled and deveined medium shrimp, thawed	12 oz.
2	lemons	1
16 oz.	dried fettuccine	8 oz.
¼ cup	olive oil	2 Tbsp.
6 cloves	garlic, thinly sliced	3 cloves
12 cups	baby spinach	6 cups
1 tsp.	Italian seasoning, crushed	½ tsp.
	Salt and black pepper	
	Fresh dill (optional)	

Shrimp and Chorizo Kabobs

The flavor of chorizo—a spicy Latin pork sausage—adds spunk to these grilled shrimp kabobs. Shrimp cook quickly and dry out easily, so watch the crustaceans carefully, removing them from the grill as soon as they begin to turn pink and opaque.

1. Thaw shrimp, if frozen. Peel and devein shrimp. Rinse shrimp; pat dry with paper towels. In a large bowl combine olive oil, ancho chile pepper, salt, chipotle chile pepper, and garlic. Mix well. Add shrimp; toss to coat. Cover bowl with plastic wrap; marinate in the refrigerator for 30 minutes (do not marinate any longer).

2. Drain shrimp, discarding marinade. Tuck 1 slice of chorizo into the crook of 1 shrimp and thread onto a 12-inch skewer (see note, page 122), making sure the skewer goes through one side of the shrimp, the chorizo, and the other side of the shrimp. Repeat with the remaining chorizo and the remaining shrimp, dividing ingredients evenly among skewers.

3. For a charcoal grill, grill kabobs on the rack of an uncovered grill directly over medium-hot coals for 4 to 6 minutes or until shrimp are opaque, turning once halfway through grilling. (For a gas grill, preheat grill. Reduce heat to medium. Add kabobs to grill rack. Cover and grill as above.)

PER SERVING *392 cal., 27 g total fat (9 g sat. fat), 210 mg chol., 1,209 mg sodium, 1 g carbo., 0 g fiber, 34 g pro.*

PREP: **20 minutes**
MARINATE: **30 minutes**
GRILL: **4 minutes**

8 servings	ingredients	4 servings
4 lb.	fresh or frozen jumbo shrimp	2 lb.
½ cup	olive oil	¼ cup
¼ cup	ground ancho chile pepper	2 Tbsp.
2 tsp.	salt	1 tsp.
¼ tsp.	ground chipotle chile pepper	⅛ tsp.
6 cloves	garlic, minced	3 cloves
24 oz.	cooked smoked chorizo sausage or spicy cooked smoked sausage, cut into ½-inch slices	12 oz.

Pacific Rim Shrimp and Snow Peas

To string snow peas for these light and fresh-tasting kabobs, just pinch the stem end and then pull the string down the flat side of the pea all the way to its pointy end.

START TO FINISH: 25 minutes

8 servings	ingredients	4 servings
24 oz.	fresh or frozen peeled and deveined medium shrimp	12 oz.
2 Tbsp.	olive oil	1 Tbsp.
16 oz.	fresh snow peas, tips and strings removed	8 oz.
6 cloves	garlic, minced	3 cloves
2 tsp.	grated fresh ginger	1 tsp.
½ tsp.	cayenne pepper	¼ tsp.
1½ cups	unsweetened coconut milk	¾ cup
1 tsp.	salt	½ tsp.
½ tsp.	finely shredded lime peel	¼ tsp.
	Hot cooked rice	
	Lime slices (optional)	

1. Thaw shrimp, if frozen. Rinse shrimp; pat dry with paper towels. Set aside.

2. In a large skillet heat oil over medium-high heat. Add snow peas; cook and stir for 2 to 3 minutes or until crisp-tender. Remove snow peas from skillet; set aside.

3. Add shrimp, garlic, ginger, and cayenne pepper to skillet. Cook and stir about 2 minutes or until shrimp turn opaque. Carefully stir in coconut milk, salt, and lime peel; heat until bubbly. Return snow peas to skillet; heat through. Serve over rice. If desired, garnish with lime slices.

PER SERVING *333 cal., 14 g total fat (9 g sat. fat), 129 mg chol., 425 mg sodium, 29 g carbo., 2 g fiber, 22 g pro.*

CHAPTER 5

Sides

These great side dishes make the rest of the meal stand up and take notice. From baked to stir-fried to tossing and roasted, these recipes provide plenty of delicious serve-alongs.

141

148

155

Pecan-Topped Apples and Carrots

When preparing fresh ginger for adding to this bright-flavor side dish, peel the ginger gently with the tip of a spoon rather than using a vegetable peeler. Ginger's most intense flavor resides just beneath its papery beige skin.

1. In a large skillet cook carrots, covered, in a small amount of boiling water for 5 minutes. Drain off liquid.

2. Add butter to carrots in skillet. Add apples, ginger, and salt. Cook, uncovered, over medium heat for 4 to 6 minutes or until carrots and apples are just tender, stirring occasionally. Add vinegar and toss to coat. Transfer to a serving dish. In a small bowl stir together pecans and parsley. Sprinkle over carrots and apples.

PER SERVING *102 cal., 5 g total fat (1 g sat. fat), 5 mg chol., 109 mg sodium, 16 g carbo., 3 g fiber, 1 g pro.*

PREP: 20 minutes
COOK: 9 minutes

8 servings	ingredients	4 servings
4	carrots, peeled and cut into bite-size strips	2
4 tsp.	butter	2 tsp.
4	red-skin cooking apples, quartered, cored, and thinly sliced	2
2 tsp.	grated fresh ginger	1 tsp.
¼ tsp.	salt	⅛ tsp.
2 Tbsp.	white wine vinegar	1 Tbsp.
¼ cup	finely chopped pecans, toasted (see note, page 102)	2 Tbsp.
2 Tbsp.	snipped fresh parsley	1 Tbsp.

Savory Pear-Hazelnut Bake

This dish is as happy to appear at breakfast as it is to take a place at the dinner table. It makes a lovely accompaniment to brunch dishes such as egg strata and is absolutely perfect paired with a simple slice of baked ham for supper.

1. Preheat oven to 375°F. In a 3-quart shallow gratin dish or individual gratin dishes combine pear slices, lemon juice, and rosemary; toss to coat. Spread in an even layer in the dish. Cover and bake for 20 to 25 minutes or until fruit is just tender.

2. Sprinkle with cheese. Bake, uncovered, 2 to 3 minutes more or until cheese is melted. Sprinkle with hazelnuts. Serve warm.

FOR 6 SERVINGS: Prepare using method above, except in Step 1 use a 1½- or 2-quart shallow gratin dish.

*TIP: To toast hazelnuts, preheat oven to 350°F. Place nuts in a shallow baking pan. Bake about 10 minutes or until toasted. Cool nuts slightly. Place the warm nuts on a clean kitchen towel. Rub the nuts with the towel to remove the loose skins.

PER SERVING 115 cal., 4 g total fat (1 g sat. fat), 2 mg chol., 58 mg sodium, 19 g carbo., 4 g fiber, 3 g pro.

PREP: 20 minutes
BAKE: 22 minutes
OVEN: 375°F

12 servings	ingredients	6 servings
8	just-ripe green- and red-skin pears, quartered, cored, and cut into ½-inch slices	4
¼ cup	lemon juice	2 Tbsp.
2 Tbsp.	snipped fresh rosemary	1 Tbsp.
½ cup	finely shredded Parmesan cheese	¼ cup
½ cup	toasted hazelnuts,* chopped	¼ cup

Sautéed Cabbage with Bacon

Not only is this sauté quick to fix, exceedingly delicious, and extra nutritious, its short cooking time ensures that your kitchen will not smell heavy with cabbage as it does when the cruciferous vegetable is slow-cooked or boiled.

1. In a large nonstick skillet cook bacon over medium heat for 5 minutes or until cooked through, stirring occasionally. Remove bacon from skillet and set aside. Add cabbage, sweet pepper, onion slices, and water to skillet. Cover and cook over medium heat for 5 minutes or until vegetables are just tender, stirring occasionally.

2. In a small bowl combine mayonnaise, mustard, vinegar, caraway seeds, and celery seeds. Add to cabbage mixture in skillet. Toss until well coated. Sprinkle with cooked bacon and serve warm.

PER SERVING *82 cal., 4 g total fat (1 g sat. fat), 10 mg chol., 255 mg sodium, 8 g carbo., 3 g fiber, 2 g pro.*

START TO FINISH: 20 minutes

8 servings	ingredients	4 servings
4 slices	turkey bacon or regular bacon, chopped	2 slices
8 cups	thinly sliced green cabbage	4 cups
2	red sweet peppers, cut into bite-size strips	1
2	onions, halved and thinly sliced	1
¼ cup	water	2 Tbsp.
¼ cup	light mayonnaise	2 Tbsp.
2 Tbsp.	course-ground mustard	1 Tbsp.
2 Tbsp.	cider vinegar	1 Tbsp.
½ tsp.	caraway seeds, crushed	¼ tsp.
½ tsp.	celery seeds	¼ tsp.

Roasted Beets with Oranges and Blue Cheese

When peeling beets, wear a pair of disposable latex gloves to protect your fingers from their crimson juices—and work over a dishwasher-safe cutting board. Beet stains are difficult to remove from wooden boards.

1. Preheat oven to 425°F. In a 3-quart square baking dish combine beets, oil, salt, and pepper. Toss to coat. Cover and roast for 20 minutes. Uncover and stir beets. Roast, uncovered, about 20 minutes more or until beets are tender.

2. Transfer beets to a serving platter. Sprinkle evenly with chopped orange and cheese.

FOR 4 SERVINGS: Prepare using method above, except in Step 1 use a 2-quart square baking dish.

PER SERVING 75 cal., 4 g total fat (1 g sat. fat), 3 mg chol., 176 mg sodium, 9 g carbo., 2 g fiber, 2 g pro.

PREP: 15 minutes
ROAST: 40 minutes
OVEN: 425°F

8 servings	ingredients	4 servings
24 oz.	trimmed small red and/or yellow beets, peeled and quartered	12 oz.
4 tsp.	canola oil	2 tsp.
¼ tsp.	salt	⅛ tsp.
¼ tsp.	black pepper	⅛ tsp.
2	Cara Cara or other navel oranges, peeled, seeded, sectioned, and chopped	1
¼ cup	crumbled blue cheese or feta cheese	2 Tbsp.

Lemon-Walnut Green Beans

Verdant fresh beans, glistening with lemon butter and spiked with crunchy walnuts, make a simple and incredibly delightful accompaniment to any fish or chicken dish.

PREP: 15 minutes
COOK: 10 minutes

8 servings	ingredients	4 servings
24 oz.	fresh green beans, trimmed	12 oz.
2 Tbsp.	vegetable oil spread	1 Tbsp.
4 tsp.	finely shredded lemon peel	2 tsp.
½ tsp.	salt	¼ tsp.
¼ cup	toasted walnuts, chopped (see note, page 102)	2 Tbsp.

1. Place a steamer basket in a large skillet with a tight-fitting lid. Add water to just below the basket. Bring water to boiling over medium-high heat. Place beans in steamer basket. Cover; steam for 8 to 10 minutes or until beans are crisp-tender. Lift steamer basket from skillet to remove the beans; set aside. Drain water from skillet.

2. In the same skillet add vegetable oil spread, lemon peel, and salt. Stir until melted and combined. Add beans to skillet. Toss to coat. Transfer to a serving dish. Sprinkle with walnuts.

PER SERVING *72 cal., 5 g total fat (1 g sat. fat), 0 mg chol., 169 mg sodium, 7 g carbo., 3 g fiber, 2 g pro.*

Glazed Carrots

The tangy-sweet flavor from the grape juice, vinegar, and honey enlivens carrots in a wonderful way. If you'd like, rinse your cinnamon stick in cool water and let air-dry—it will be good for several more uses before its flavor dissipates.

1. Peel large carrots. Slice carrots lengthwise and/or crosswise. Heat a large skillet over medium-high heat. Add white grape juice, vinegar, honey, butter, salt, cinnamon, and bay leaves. Bring to boiling, stirring to combine. Add carrots; return to boiling. Reduce heat to medium. Cook, uncovered, 25 minutes, stirring often, until carrots are tender and glaze thickens.

2. Remove from heat. Remove and discard cinnamon stick and bay leaves. Sprinkle with chives.

PER SERVING *156 cal., 3 g total fat (2 g sat. fat), 8 mg chol., 314 mg sodium, 28 g carbo., 3 g fiber, 1 g pro.*

PREP: 15 minutes
COOK: 25 minutes

8 servings	ingredients	4 servings
2 lbs.	assorted carrots	1 lb.
¾ cup	white grape juice	⅓ cup
¼ cup	white wine vinegar	2 Tbsp.
½ cup	honey	¼ cup
2 Tbsp.	unsalted butter	1 Tbsp.
1 tsp.	kosher salt	½ tsp.
2	cinnamon sticks	1
2	bay leaves	1
2 Tbsp.	sliced chives	1 Tbsp.

Pan-Roasted Mushrooms

Serve these magnificent mushrooms in small individual ramekins or, ladle them over any simple grilled or broiled steak or chicken. Look for interesting, prepackaged collections of various mushrooms.

1. In a large skillet cook mushrooms and onion in hot oil over medium heat for 10 to 12 minutes or until tender and golden brown, stirring occasionally. Add garlic; cook and stir for 30 seconds. Remove from heat. Carefully add vinegar, thyme, salt, and pepper. Toss to coat.

PER SERVING *69 cal., 3 g total fat (0 g sat. fat), 0 mg chol., 153 mg sodium, 7 g carbo., 1 g fiber, 2 g pro.*

PREP: 15 minutes
COOK: 11 minutes

8 servings	ingredients	4 servings
24 oz.	fresh mushrooms (such as cremini, stemmed shiitake, and/or button), halved	12 oz.
1 cup	chopped red onion	½ cup
2 Tbsp.	olive oil	1 Tbsp.
4 cloves	garlic, minced	2 cloves
¼ cup	balsamic vinegar	2 Tbsp.
2 Tbsp.	snipped fresh thyme	1 Tbsp.
½ tsp.	salt	¼ tsp.
¼ tsp.	black pepper	⅛ tsp.

Butternut Squash-Wild Rice Casserole

Before you purchase a whole butternut squash, check your grocer's shelves for precubed butternut squash. Usually shelved along with other ready-to-go veggies, it comes in 8-ounce packages, that will save you a ton of labor.

PREP: 30 minutes
ROAST: 20 minutes   BAKE: 45 minutes
OVEN: 425°F/350°F

10 servings	ingredients	5 servings
16 oz.	butternut squash, peeled, seeded, and cut into ½-inch cubes	8 oz.
1 to 2 Tbsp.	olive oil	1½ to 3 tsp.
2 6-oz. pkg.	long grain and wild rice mix	1 6-oz. pkg.
¾ cup	chopped onions	⅓ cup
¾ cup	chopped celery	⅓ cup
¾ cup	chopped carrots	⅓ cup
⅓ cup	butter	2 Tbsp.
2 10.5-oz. cans	condensed chicken with white and wild rice soup or cream of chicken soup	1 10.5-oz. can
1 8-oz. carton	sour cream	½ 8-oz. carton
⅔ cup	dry white wine or chicken broth	⅓ cup
¼ cup	snipped fresh basil	2 Tbsp.
1½ cups	finely shredded Parmesan cheese	¾ cup

1. Preheat oven to 425°F. In a large bowl toss squash with oil to coat; spread into a 15×10×1-inch baking pan. Roast about 20 minutes or until lightly browned and tender, stirring twice. Reduce oven temperature to 350°F.

2. Meanwhile, prepare rice mix according to package directions; set aside. In a large skillet cook onions, celery, and carrots in hot butter over medium heat until tender. Stir in soup, sour cream, wine, and basil. Stir in cooked rice mix, roasted squash, and ¾ cup of the Parmesan cheese.

3. Transfer rice mixture to a 2½- to 3-quart casserole. Sprinkle with the remaining ¾ cup Parmesan cheese. Bake for 45 to 50 minutes or until heated through and top is browned.

FOR 5 SERVINGS: Prepare using method above, except in Step 2 use half the ¾ cup Parmesan cheese. In Step 3 use a 1½-quart square baking dish and sprinkle with remaining Parmesan cheese.

PER SERVING *357 cal., 16 g total fat (9 g sat. fat), 39 mg chol., 1136 mg sodium, 42 g carbo., 3 g fiber, 11 g pro.*

Loaded Creamed Corn with Tomato and Bacon

When preparing big, oven-intensive meals, slow cookers is smart way to save space and reduce last-minute preparation: This cheesy corn dish is always a winner and is perfect for toting to potluck dinners.

1. In a blender combine the corn from 1 package and the half-and-half. Cover and blend until smooth. In a 3½- or 4-quart slow cooker combine blended corn mixture, the remaining corn, the onion, Parmesan cheese, butter, the 1 teaspoon sugar, the salt, and pepper.

2. Cover and cook on low-heat setting for 3 to 4 hours or on high-heat setting for 1½ to 2 hours.

3. In a skillet cook bacon over medium heat until crisp, turning once. Drain bacon on paper towels; cool. Cut bacon into 1-inch pieces.

4. Sprinkle Monterey Jack cheese and bacon over corn in slow cooker. Cover; let stand for about 5 minutes or until cheese is melted. Stir to combine.

5. In a small bowl stir together tomato, parsley, vinegar, and the ⅛ teaspoon sugar. Transfer corn to a serving bowl. Spoon tomato mixture over corn.

FOR 8 SERVINGS: Prepare using method above, except in Step 1 use a 1½- to 2-quart slow cooker and the ½ teaspoon sugar. In Step 5 use the dash of sugar.

PER SERVING 186 cal., 10 g total fat (6 g sat. fat), 27 mg chol., 258 mg sodium, 20 g carbo., 2 g fiber, 7 g pro.

PREP: 25 minutes
SLOW COOK: 3 hours (low) or 1½ hours (high)
STAND: 5 minutes

16 servings	ingredients	8 servings
4 12-oz. pkg.	frozen whole kernel corn, thawed	2 12-oz. pkg.
1½ cups	half-and-half or light cream	¾ cup
1 cup	chopped onion	½ cup
½ cup	freshly grated Parmesan cheese	¼ cup
¼ cup	butter, cut up	2 Tbsp.
1 tsp.	sugar	½ tsp.
½ tsp.	salt	¼ tsp.
¼ tsp.	black pepper	⅛ tsp.
5 thick slices	bacon	2 thick slices
¾ cup	shredded Monterey Jack cheese with jalapeño peppers or Monterey Jack cheese	⅓ cup
½ cup	chopped tomato	¼ cup
2 Tbsp.	snipped fresh parsley	1 Tbsp.
1 tsp.	red wine vinegar	½ tsp.
⅛ tsp.	sugar	dash

Creamy Brie-Topped Potatoes

This luxurious, dairy-rich potato bake is heaven in a dish. Consider serving it with lean meat, such as filet mignons or marinated and thinly sliced tri-tip steaks.

1. Preheat oven to 350°F. Grease a 2-quart gratin dish or rectangular baking dish; set aside. In a covered Dutch oven cook potatoes in enough simmering salted water to cover for 25 minutes; drain. Rinse with cold water; drain again. Slice potatoes about ¼ inch thick. Sprinkle with salt and pepper. Place half of the potatoes in the prepared dish.

2. Meanwhile, in a large skillet cook bacon over medium heat for 1 minute. Add onion and garlic; cook and stir about 5 minutes or until bacon is crisp and onion is tender. Drain off fat. Carefully add wine to bacon mixture. Simmer, uncovered, until wine is almost evaporated. Stir in the snipped thyme.

3. Spoon bacon mixture over potatoes in dish. Top with the remaining potatoes. Pour broth and cream over potato mixture. Cut Brie crosswise into ¼-inch-thick rectangles and layer on potato mixture.

4. Bake about 40 minutes or until potatoes are tender and cheese is lightly browned. If desired, garnish with fresh thyme sprigs.

FOR 6 SERVINGS: Prepare using method above, except in Step 1 use a 1-quart gratin or baking dish

PER SERVING *267 cal., 15 g total fat (8 g sat. fat), 49 mg chol., 468 mg sodium, 22 g carbo., 3 g fiber, 12 g pro.*

PREP: 45 minutes
BAKE: 40 minutes
OVEN: 350°F

12 servings	ingredients	6 servings
3 lb.	Yukon gold potatoes	1½ lb.
½ tsp.	salt	¼ tsp.
¼ tsp.	black pepper	⅛ tsp.
5 slices	thick-sliced bacon, chopped	2 slices
1 large	onion, thinly sliced	1 small
2 cloves	garlic, minced	1 clove
⅓ cup	dry white wine	2 Tbsp.
2 tsp.	snipped fresh thyme	1 tsp.
¼ cup	chicken broth	2 Tbsp.
¼ cup	whipping cream	2 Tbsp.
2 8-oz. rounds	Brie cheese	1 8-oz. round
	Fresh thyme sprigs (optional)	

Cauliflower-Fontina Gratin

Fontina—a mild, buttery, nutty-flavor cheese—is a delectable duo with cauliflower. If you're unable to find Fontina, mild provolone, Gruyère or Gouda cheese will stand in admirably.

PREP: 30 minutes
BAKE: 25 minutes
OVEN: 375°F

12 servings	ingredients	6 servings
6 cups	cauliflower florets	3 cups
¼ cup	butter	2 Tbsp.
¼ cup	all-purpose flour	2 Tbsp.
2 cups	half-and-half, light cream, or milk	1 cup
½ cup	milk	¼ cup
¾ cup	shredded Fontina cheese	⅓ cup
1 Tbsp.	snipped fresh thyme	1½ tsp.
½ tsp.	salt	¼ tsp.
¼ tsp.	black pepper	⅛ tsp.
⅔ cup	soft bread crumbs	⅓ cup
2 Tbsp.	olive oil	1 Tbsp.
	Snipped fresh thyme (optional)	

1. Preheat oven to 375°F. Grease a 2-quart square baking dish; set aside. In a Dutch oven cook cauliflower in boiling lightly salted water about 5 minutes or just until tender; drain. Transfer to a bowl of ice water to stop cooking. Drain again; set aside.

2. For the cheese sauce, in a medium saucepan melt butter over medium-low heat. Stir in flour. Cook and stir for 1 minute. Stir in half-and-half and the ½ cup milk. Cook and stir over medium heat until thickened and bubbly. Cook and stir for 1 minute more. Remove from heat. Stir in Fontina cheese, the 1 tablespoon fresh thyme, the salt, and pepper.

3. Spread about 1 cup of the cheese sauce evenly in the bottom of the prepared dish. Arrange cauliflower florets in an even layer in the baking dish. Spread the remaining sauce over the cauliflower.

4. Sprinkle gratin evenly with bread crumbs; drizzle evenly with olive oil. Bake for 25 to 30 minutes or until lightly browned and bubbly. If desired, sprinkle with additional snipped fresh thyme.

FOR 6 SERVINGS: Prepare using method above, except in Step 1 use a 1-quart square baking dish. In Step 2 use ¼ cup milk and 1½ teaspoons fresh thyme.

PER SERVING *167 cal., 13 g total fat (7 g sat. fat), 34 mg chol., 234 mg sodium, 8 g carbo., 1 g fiber, 5 g pro.*

Easy Pommes Anna-Style Casserole

Exquisitely thin-sliced potatoes combine with smoky bacon, butter, and garlic to form a beautiful compressed potato cake worthy of the finest meal. Yukon gold potatoes contain the right amount of starch to make this dish bind together beautifully.

1. Scrub or peel potatoes. Using a mandoline, slice potatoes about ⅛ inch thick. Layer half the potatoes in the bottom of a 3½- to 4-quart slow cooker. Sprinkle with half the salt and half of the pepper. Sprinkle with half the chopped green onions, half the bacon, and half the garlic. Repeat layers. Drizzle evenly with butter.

2. Cover and cook on low-heat setting for 5½ to 6 hours or until potatoes are tender when pierced with a fork. Loosen edges with a spatula. Garnish with the sliced green onions.

FOR 6 SERVINGS: Prepare using method above, except in Step 1 use a 1½- to 2-quart slow cooker.

PER SERVING 203 cal., 12 g total fat (7 g sat. fat), 32 mg chol., 334 mg sodium, 21 g carbo., 3 g fiber, 4 g pro.

PREP: 25 minutes
SLOW COOK: 5½ hours (low)

12 servings	ingredients	6 servings
3 lb.	Yukon gold potatoes	1½ lb.
1 tsp.	kosher salt or salt	½ tsp.
½ tsp.	coarse-ground black pepper	¼ tsp.
¾ cup	chopped green onions	⅓ cup
6 slices	bacon, crisp-cooked and crumbled	3 slices
3 cloves	garlic, minced	1 clove
⅔ cup	melted butter	⅓ cup
	Sliced green onions	

Mandarin Orange Salad

Sticky-note this page so this recipe is easy to locate at Eastertime. In a matter of minutes, you will have a light, lovely salad that will grace the holiday table with its beautiful palette of spring colors.

1. In a screw-top jar combine the vinegar, orange juice, oil, sugar, and mustard. Cover and shake well.

2. Place greens in a large salad bowl. Pour dressing over salad. Toss gently to coat. Arrange orange sections and raspberries over greens. Sprinkle with almonds.

PER SERVING *89 cal., 5 g total fat (1 g sat. fat), 0 mg chol., 10 mg sodium, 10 g carbo., 2 g fiber, 2 g pro.*

START TO FINISH: 20 minutes

12 servings	ingredients	6 servings
2 Tbsp.	red wine vinegar	1 Tbsp.
2 Tbsp.	orange juice	1 Tbsp.
2 Tbsp.	olive oil	1 Tbsp.
2 tsp.	sugar	1 tsp.
½ tsp.	dry mustard	¼ tsp.
12 cups	mixed greens	6 cups
2 10.5-oz. cans	mandarin orange sections (juice pack), drained	1 10.5-oz. can
1 cup	fresh raspberries	½ cup
½ cup	sliced almonds, lightly toasted (see note, page 102)	¼ cup

Persimmon, Blood Orange, and Pomegranate Salad

Short, plump, squat Fuyu persimmons ripen in late fall and usually arrive on grocers' shelves by mid-November. The fruit is mildly sweet with a hint of cinnamon flavor, a crisp texture, and may be eaten just like an apple.

1. Score an "X" into the top of the pomegranate. Break apart into quarters. Working in a bowl of cool water, immerse each quarter; use your fingers to loosen the seeds from the white membrane. Discard peel and membrane. Drain the seeds; set aside.

2. Cut each persimmon in half; remove core. Slice into ¼- to ½-inch-thick slices.

3. In a large bowl combine mesclun and green onions. Drizzle 1 cup of the Pine Nut-Persimmon Vinaigrette over mesclun; toss to coat.

4. To serve, arrange mesclun mixture on six chilled salad plates. Arrange persimmons and oranges on greens, tucking a few in and under leaves. Sprinkle with pomegranate seeds. Pass the remaining Pine Nut-Persimmon Vinaigrette.

PINE NUT-PERSIMMON VINAIGRETTE: Remove the core from 1 large ripe Fuyu persimmon; cut in half. Scoop out pulp (you should have about ⅓ cup), discarding skin. Place pulp in a blender or food processor. Cover and blend or process until smooth. Add ⅓ cup olive oil; ¼ cup red or white wine vinegar; 3 tablespoons toasted pine nuts; 1½ teaspoons finely shredded blood orange peel or orange peel; 2 tablespoons blood orange juice or orange juice; 1 tablespoon honey; ½ of a large shallot, cut up; ½ teaspoon Dijon mustard; dash ground cinnamon or ground allspice; and dash freshly ground black pepper. Cover and blend or process until smooth.

FOR 6 SERVINGS: Prepare using method above, except in Step 3 drizzle ½ cup of the Pine Nut-Persimmon Vinaigrette over mesclun; toss to coat.

PER SERVING 238 cal., 15 g total fat (2 g sat. fat), 0 mg chol., 18 mg sodium, 26 g carbo., 3 g fiber, 2 g pro.

START TO FINISH: **50 minutes**

12 servings	ingredients	6 servings
2	pomegranate	1
4 large	ripe Fuyu persimmons, mangoes, or papayas	2 large
10 cups	mesclun, arugula, baby arugula, or mixed salad greens	5 cups
¾ cup	thinly sliced green onions	6 Tbsp.
2 recipes	Pine Nut-Persimmon Vinaigrette	1 recipe
8 medium	blood and/or navel oranges, peeled and thinly sliced	4 medium

Romaine and Radicchio Salad

Bold and assertive, this colorful, crisp concoction is welcome alongside roasted chicken, broiled fish, and grilled pork.

START TO FINISH: 20 minutes

8 servings	ingredients	4 servings
10 cups	torn romaine or mixed salad greens	5 cups
2 cups	torn radicchio	1 cup
⅓ cup	olive oil	2 Tbsp.
¼ cup	white wine vinegar	2 Tbsp.
4	anchovy fillets, drained and finely chopped	2
¼ tsp.	salt	⅛ tsp.
½ tsp.	freshly ground black pepper	¼ tsp.
1 cup	finely shredded Parmesan cheese	½ cup

1. In a large bowl combine romaine and radicchio.

2. For the dressing, in a medium bowl whisk together oil, vinegar, anchovies, salt, and pepper until thoroughly combined. Drizzle dressing over romaine mixture. Add Parmesan cheese; toss gently to coat. Serve immediately.

PER SERVING *155 cal., 13 g total fat (4 g sat. fat), 10 mg chol., 350 mg sodium, 4 g carbo. 2 g fiber, 7 g pro.*

Wilted Spinach Salad with Pears and Cranberries

This bright green, ruby-studded salad is sensational served with baked ham or roasted turkey. If you decide to tear large spinach leaves for the salad, be sure to remove any large stems.

1. Place pears in a bowl; drizzle with lemon juice. Fill bowl with enough water to cover pears. Place a small plate over pears to submerge pears; set aside. In a large bowl combine spinach and red onion. If desired, sprinkle with pepper; set aside.

2. For dressing, in a Dutch oven cook bacon until crisp. Remove bacon, reserving ½ cup drippings in Dutch oven. (If necessary, add enough oil to equal ¼ cup.) Crumble bacon; set aside. Stir the 1 cup cranberries, the vinegar, sugar, and mustard into drippings in Dutch oven. Bring to boiling; remove from heat. Add spinach mixture. Toss mixture in skillet for 30 to 60 seconds or just until spinach is wilted.

3. Transfer spinach mixture to a large bowl. Add bacon; toss to combine. Divide spinach mixture among 12 salad plates; drain pears and arrange on top of spinach mixture. If desired, sprinkle with Gorgonzola cheese and additional cranberries.

FOR 6 SERVINGS: Prepare using method above, except in Step 2 reserve ¼ cup drippings in Dutch oven and use the ½ cup cranberries. In Step 3 divide spinach mixture among 6 salad plates.

PER SERVING *214 cal., 11 g total fat (4 g sat. fat), 14 mg chol., 225 mg sodium, 25 g carbo., 5 g fiber, 5 g pro.*

START TO FINISH: 35 minutes

12 servings	ingredients	6 servings
4 medium	pears, cored and thinly sliced	2 medium
¼ cup	lemon juice	2 Tbsp.
24 cups	packaged fresh baby spinach or torn spinach	12 cups
1½ cups	thinly sliced red onion	¾ cup
	Dash black pepper (optional)	
8 slices	bacon	4 slices
	Vegetable oil (optional)	
1 cup	dried cranberries	½ cup
⅔ cup	red wine vinegar	⅓ cup
2 Tbsp.	sugar	1 Tbsp.
1 tsp.	dry mustard	½ tsp.
	Gorgonzola cheese, crumbled (optional)	
	Dried cranberries (optional)	

Wild Rice, Barley, and Dried Cherry Pilaf

For an upcoming holiday meal, opt for this baked toothsome blend of chewy grains, tart cherries, and crunchy pecans. The earthy fall flavors make an extraordinary match for roasted turkey.

1. Preheat oven to 325°F. Place rice in a pan of warm water, stir, and remove particles that float to the top. Drain and rinse again.

2. In a saucepan combine rice and chicken broth. Bring to boiling; reduce heat. Cover and simmer for 10 minutes. Remove from heat. Stir in barley, cherries, marjoram, and butter. Spoon into a 3-quart casserole.

3. Bake, covered, for 60 to 65 minutes or until rice and barley are tender and liquid is absorbed, stirring once. Fluff rice mixture with a fork; stir in pecans. Season to taste with salt and pepper.

FOR 6 SERVINGS: Prepare using method above, except in Step 2 use a 1½-quart casserole.

PER SERVING *279 cal., 9 g total fat (3 g sat. fat), 12 mg chol., 658 mg sodium, 44 g carbo., 7 g fiber, 8 g pro.*

PREP: 10 minutes   BAKE: 1 hour
COOK: 10 minutes   OVEN: 325°F

12 servings	ingredients	6 servings
1½ cups	uncooked wild rice	¾ cup
4 14-oz. cans	chicken broth	2 14-oz. cans
1½ cups	regular barley	¾ cup
1 cup	snipped dried cherries or apricots, or dried cranberries	½ cup
1½ tsp.	dried marjoram or dried oregano, crushed	¾ tsp.
¼ cup	butter	2 Tbsp.
⅔ cup	coarsely chopped pecans, toasted	⅓ cup
	Salt and black pepper	

Figgy Brie Rolls

These tender whole wheat rolls contain a surprise—a hidden center of sticky figs and creamy Brie cheese. To make sticky figs a bit easier to chop, dip your knife in warm water occasionally.

PREP: 25 minutes   RISE: 1 hour
BAKE: 20 minutes   COOL: 5 minutes
OVEN: 350°F

24 servings	ingredients	12 servings
⅔ cup	finely chopped dried figs	⅓ cup
2 tsp.	snipped fresh sage	1 tsp.
2 tsp.	honey	1 tsp.
2 16-oz. loaves	frozen wheat bread dough, thawed	1 16-oz. loaf
4 oz.	Brie cheese, cut into ½-inch pieces	2 oz.
2	egg whites	1
2 Tbsp.	water	1 Tbsp.
	Small fresh sage leaves	

1. Line a 13×9×2-inch baking pan with foil. Grease foil; set aside. For filling, in a small bowl combine figs, snipped sage, and honey; set aside.

2. Cut dough into 24 equal portions. Shape dough portions into balls. Working with one dough ball at a time, flatten it to a 3-inch circle. Top with a rounded teaspoon of the filling and a few pieces of the cheese. Fold dough over filling; pinch edges to seal. Place rolls, seam sides down, in the prepared baking pan. Cover and let rise until double in size (1 to 1¼ hours).

3. Preheat oven to 350°F. In a small bowl whisk together egg white and the water; brush lightly over rolls. Gently press small sage leaves onto tops of rolls; brush again with egg white mixture.

4. Bake about 20 minutes or until golden. Cool in pan on a wire rack for 5 minutes. Serve warm.

FOR 12 SERVINGS: Prepare using method above, except in Step 1 use a 9×9×2-inch baking pan. In Step 2 cut dough into 12 equal portions.

PER SERVING *127 cal., 3 g total fat (1 g sat. fat), 5 mg chol., 245 mg sodium, 21 g carbo., 2 g fiber, 6 g pro.*

Brandy-Soaked Currant, Thyme, and Parmesan Scones

Coffeehouse culture has us accustomed to sweet scones, but the rich, biscuitlike quick breads are wonderful when prepared with savory ingredients such as herbs and cheese. Serve these with a bowls of homemade soup for a real treat.

1. Line two baking sheets with parchment paper.

2. In a small saucepan combine currants and brandy. Heat over medium heat just until warm. Remove from heat. Cover and let stand for 15 minutes. Drain.

3. In a food processor* combine flour, 1 cup of the cheese, the baking powder, sugar, thyme, pepper, and salt; cover and pulse with several on/off turns to combine. Sprinkle butter pieces over flour mixture; cover and pulse with several on/off turns until mixture resembles coarse crumbs. Add drained currants; cover and pulse with several on/off turns to combine. With the motor running, slowly add whipping cream through the feed tube, processing just until combined.

4. Turn out dough onto a lightly floured surface. Knead dough by folding and gently pressing for 10 to 12 strokes or just until dough holds together. Pat or roll the dough to two 8-inch circles, about ¾ inch thick. In a bowl whisk together egg and the water; brush over dough circles. Sprinkle with the remaining ½ cup cheese. Using floured sharp knife, cut each dough circle into eight wedges. Place the 2 dough circles on baking sheets, wedges set slightly apart. Cover; chill for 30 minutes.

5. Preheat oven to 375°F. Bake about 20 minutes or until golden. Serve warm.

FOR 8 SERVINGS: Prepare using method above, except in Step 1 use one baking sheet. In Step 3 use ½ cup of the cheese. In Step 4 pat dough into one 8-inch circle and use ¼ cup cheese.

*__NOTE__ If you don't have a food processor, in a large bowl use a pastry blender to cut the butter into the flour mixture until the mixture resembles coarse crumbs.

PER SERVING 311 cal., 16 g total fat (10 g sat. fat), 75 mg chol., 467 mg sodium, 31 g carbo., 1 g fiber, 7 g pro.

PREP: 25 minutes   STAND: 15 minutes
CHILL: 30 minutes   BAKE: 20 minutes
OVEN: 375°F

16 servings	ingredients	8 servings
1 cup	dried currants	½ cup
½ cup	brandy or apple juice	¼ cup
2½ cups	all-purpose flour	1¾ cups
1½ cups	finely shredded Parmigiano-Reggiano cheese	¾ cup
2 Tbsp.	baking powder	1 Tbsp.
2 Tbsp.	sugar	1 Tbsp.
2 Tbsp.	finely snipped fresh thyme	1 Tbsp.
2 tsp.	freshly ground black pepper	1 tsp.
1 tsp.	salt	½ tsp.
½ cup	cold butter, cut into small pieces	¼ cup
1⅓ cups	whipping cream	⅔ cup
2	egg	1
2 Tbsp.	water	1 Tbsp.

Brandied Blue Cheese Bread

This quick-to-fix bread makes an extraordinary accompaniment to grilled steaks. Choose any blue-veined cheese that you like—creamy Danish blue, crumbly American blue, tangy Gorgonzola, and even over-the-top Stilton all work wonderfully.

1. Preheat oven to 350°F. Use a serrated knife to cut bread crosswise into 1-inch slices, cutting to, but not through, the bottom crust.

2. In a small bowl stir together butter, cheese, chives, brandy (if desired), and cayenne pepper. Spread mixture between slices of bread. Wrap loaves in foil.

3. Bake for 10 to 15 minutes or until bread is heated through and cheese is melted.

FOR 12 SERVINGS: Prepare using method above, except in Step 2 wrap the 1 loaf in foil.

PER SERVING 166 cal., 10 g total fat (6 g sat. fat), 24 mg chol., 305 mg sodium, 16 g carbo., 1 g fiber, 5 g pro.

PREP: **10 minutes**
BAKE: **10 minutes**
OVEN: **350°F**

24 servings	ingredients	12 servings
2 12- to 16-oz. loaves	baguette-style French bread	1 12- to 16-oz. loaf
1 cup	butter, softened	½ cup
1 4-oz. pkg.	crumbled blue cheese	½ 4-oz. pkg.
2 Tbsp.	snipped fresh chives	1 Tbsp.
2 Tbsp.	brandy (optional)	1 Tbsp.
¼ tsp.	cayenne pepper	⅛ tsp.

CHAPTER 6

Desserts

One of the best ways to win friends and influence people is to serve them sweets. With this time-tested collection of cakes, bars, and crisps, you'll be serving sweets with style—and creating smiles and satisfying everyone's sweet tooth along the way.

161

169

187

Sweet Potato-Buttermilk Pound Cake

Raw, shredded sweet potato—skin and all—graces this luscious cake with a sprinkling of bright yellow-orange confetti, making it a stunner of an autumn dessert. When using buttermilk, shake the carton well before measuring.

PREP: 30 minutes   STAND: 30 minutes
BAKE: 1 hour 5 minutes   COOL: 2 hours
OVEN: 350°F

24 servings	ingredients	12 servings
6	eggs	3
1 cup	buttermilk	½ cup
4 cups	all-purpose flour	2 cups
2 tsp.	baking powder	1 tsp.
2 tsp.	ground cinnamon	1 tsp.
1 tsp.	baking soda	½ tsp.
½ tsp.	salt	¼ tsp.
½ tsp.	ground allspice	¼ tsp.
½ tsp.	ground nutmeg	¼ tsp.
1½ cup	butter, cut into pieces	¾ cup
2 cups	sugar	1 cup
2 tsp.	vanilla	1 tsp.
4 cups	shredded, unpeeled sweet potatoes	2 cups

1. Allow eggs and buttermilk to stand at room temperature for 30 minutes. Meanwhile, preheat oven to 350°F. Grease and lightly flour two 9×5×3-inch loaf pans; set aside. In a medium bowl stir together flour, baking powder, cinnamon, baking soda, salt, allspice, and nutmeg; set aside.

2. In a large microwave-safe bowl microwave butter on low for 1½ to 2½ minutes or until very soft but not melted, checking and turning bowl every 30 seconds. Whisk in sugar until combined. Add eggs, one at a time, whisking well after each addition. Whisk in buttermilk and vanilla (mixture might look curdled). Whisk in flour mixture until smooth. Fold in sweet potatoes. Pour batter into the prepared pans, spreading evenly.

3. Bake for 65 to 70 minutes or until tops spring back when lightly touched and cracks look dry. Cool in pan on a wire rack for 10 minutes. Remove from pans; cool completely.

FOR 12 SERVINGS: Prepare using method above, except in Step 1 use one 9×5×3-inch loaf pan.

PER SERVING 295 cal., 13 g total fat (8 g sat. fat), 84 mg chol., 245 mg sodium, 41 g carbo., 2 g fiber, 5 g pro.

Butterscotch Chip Oatmeal Cake

A mere teaspoon of finely grated orange peel is all it takes to bring out the old-fashioned flavors in this easy cake. When grating the peel, be sure to remove just the thin, outermost orange skin—the pith beneath it can be quite bitter.

1. Preheat oven to 350°F. In a large bowl pour the boiling water over oats; let stand for 10 minutes. Meanwhile, grease and lightly flour a 13×9×2-inch baking pan; set aside.

2. Add granulated sugar, brown sugar, and butter to oats mixture, stirring until butter is melted. Stir in eggs until combined. Stir in flour, baking soda, orange peel, and salt until combined. Stir in 1 cup of the butterscotch pieces.

3. Pour batter into the prepared baking pan, spreading evenly. Sprinkle with pecans and the remaining butterscotch pieces. Bake about 40 minutes or until a wooden toothpick inserted near the center comes out clean. Cool in pan on a wire rack.

FOR 10 SERVINGS: Prepare using method above, except in Step 1 use an 8×8×2-inch baking pan. In Step 2 use 1 egg and ½ cup of the butterscotch pieces.

PER SERVING *294 cal., 13 g total fat (6 g sat. fat), 33 mg chol., 167 mg sodium, 43 g carbo., 2 g fiber, 4 g pro.*

PREP: 25 minutes   STAND: 10 minutes
BAKE: 40 minutes
OVEN: 350°F

20 servings	ingredients	10 servings
1¾ cups	boiling water	¾ cup + 2 Tbsp.
1 cup	quick-cooking rolled oats	½ cup
1 cup	granulated sugar	½ cup
1 cup	packed brown sugar	½ cup
½ cup	butter, cut up and softened	¼ cup
2	eggs	1
1¾ cups	all-purpose flour	¾ cup + 2 Tbsp.
1 tsp.	baking soda	½ tsp.
1 tsp.	finely shredded orange peel	½ tsp.
½ tsp.	salt	¼ tsp.
1 11-oz. pkg.	butterscotch-flavor pieces	½ 11-oz. pkg
¾ cup	chopped pecans	⅓ cup

Flourless Chocolate-Pecan Cake

Trufflelike in texture and incredibly rich, this flour-free cake brings pastry-shop-special elegance and sophistication to the dessert plates—and it's ready for "oohs" and "ahhs" in just over an hour.

1. Preheat oven to 350°F. Grease two 9×1½-inch round cake pans. Line bottom of pans with waxed paper; grease the paper. Set pans aside.

2. In a blender or food processor combine pecans, sugar, chopped chocolate, cocoa powder, baking powder, and baking soda. Cover; blend or process until nuts are ground. Add eggs and vanilla. Blend or process until nearly smooth. Pour batter into prepared pans, spreading evenly.

3. Bake about 30 minutes or until a wooden toothpick inserted near centers of cakes comes out clean. Cool in pans on a wire rack for 10 minutes. Remove cakes from pans; peel off waxed paper. Cool thoroughly on wire rack.

4. To serve, cut each cake into 16 wedges. Place one wedge on each dessert plate and drizzle with sauce. Place another wedge on top at an angle. Drizzle with more sauce.

TOASTED COCONUT-PECAN CARAMEL SAUCE: Spread 1 cup flaked coconut and 1 cup chopped pecans in a thin layer in a shallow baking pan. Bake in a 350°F oven for 6 to 8 minutes or until coconut is toasted and nuts are golden brown, stirring once or twice. Remove from oven. In a medium bowl stir together two 12.25-ounce jars caramel ice cream topping (room temperature), the coconut, and pecans.

FOR 8 SERVINGS: Prepare using method above, except in Step 1 use one 9×1½-inch round cake pan.

PER SERVING 526 cal., 28 g total fat (5 g sat. fat), 133 mg chol., 269 mg sodium, 63 g carbo., 4 g fiber, 8 g pro.

PREP: 30 minutes
BAKE: 30 minutes
COOL: 10 minutes
OVEN: 350°F

16 servings	ingredients	8 servings
3 cups	broken pecans	1½ cups
1½ cups	sugar	¾ cup
⅔ cup	coarsely chopped sweet baking chocolate	⅓ cup
½ cup	unsweetened Dutch-process cocoa powder or unsweetened cocoa powder	¼ cup
2 tsp.	baking powder	1 tsp.
½ tsp.	baking soda	¼ tsp.
10	eggs	5
3 tsp.	vanilla	1½ tsp.
1 recipe	Toasted Coconut-Pecan Caramel Sauce	½ recipe

Pineapple Upside-Down Coffee Cake

Say aloha to a quick, simple, and sunny-looking cake guaranteed to brighten morning coffee. Pineapple has a special affinity for nutmeg. Make the most of the dynamite duo by using freshly ground nutmeg.

PREP: 25 minutes BAKE: 35 minutes
OVEN: 350°F

12 servings	ingredients	6 servings
½ cup (1 stick)	butter	¼ cup (½ stick)
1 cup	packed brown sugar	½ cup
12	canned pineapple rings in juice	6
12	stemmed maraschino cherries	6
2 cups	all-purpose flour	1 cup
2 tsp.	baking powder	1 tsp.
½ tsp.	salt	¼ tsp.
½ tsp.	ground nutmeg	¼ tsp.
½ cup (1 stick)	butter, softened	¼ cup (½ stick)
½ cup	granulated sugar	¼ cup
½ cup	packed brown sugar	¼ cup
2	eggs	1
½ cup	milk	¼ cup
1 tsp.	vanilla	½ tsp.
	Vanilla Greek yogurt or sweetened whipped cream (optional)	
1 Tbsp.	packed brown sugar (optional)	1½ tsp.

1. Preheat oven to 350°F. Butter the bottom and sides of a 13×9×2-inch baking pan. Line bottom of pan with parchment paper; set pan aside. For topping, melt ½ cup butter in a medium saucepan on stovetop over low heat. Stir in 1 cup brown sugar. Bring mixture to boiling over medium heat, stirring frequently. Pour into prepared pan. Drain pineapple rings, reserving ½ cup juice. Fit rings tightly into bottom of pan. Place 1 maraschino cherry in each pineapple ring.

2. In a medium bowl whisk together flour, baking powder, salt, and nutmeg. In a large bowl beat softened butter, granulated sugar, and ½ cup brown sugar with an electric mixer on medium for 2 minutes, scraping sides of bowl occasionally. Add eggs; beat until combined. Beat in half the flour mixture. Pour in reserved ½ cup pineapple juice and the milk; beat until combined. Beat in remaining flour mixture and vanilla.

3. Spread batter carefully over pineapple slices in pan. Bake for 35 to 40 minutes or until toothpick inserted in center comes out clean. Cool cake in pan on wire rack 10 minutes. If you rush to pop the cake out too soon, the pineapple rings may stick to the pan. Allow the full 10 minutes for cooling. Place a baking sheet over cake; carefully invert. If any pineapple sticks to pan, gently replace on cake top.

4. Meanwhile, if desired, in a small bowl stir together the yogurt and 1 tablespoon brown sugar. Serve cake warm topped with yogurt mixture.

FOR 6 SERVINGS: Prepare using method above, except in Step 1 use an 8×8×2-inch baking pan. Reserve ¼ cup juice. In Step 2 use ¼ cup brown sugar. Pour in reserved ¼ cup juice.

PER SERVING 396 cal., 17 g total fat (10 g sat. fat), 77 mg chol., 290 mg sodium, 60 g carbo., 1 g fiber, 4 g pro.

Crumb-Topped Cherry Coffee Cake

The problem with this recipe is deciding when it should be served. Its ruby cherries make it a perfect choice for the holidays and Valentine's Day, but its utter deliciousness will also brighten breakfast or brunch any timer.

PREP: 35 minutes   BAKE: 1 hour
COOL: 30 minutes
OVEN: 350°F

16 servings	ingredients	8 servings
	Nonstick cooking spray	
1 16-oz. carton	sour cream	1 8-oz. carton
2 tsp.	baking soda	1 tsp.
4 cups	all-purpose flour	2 cups
1 Tbsp.	baking powder	1½ tsp.
1 cup	packed brown sugar	½ cup
½ cup	chopped walnuts	¼ cup
4½ tsp.	ground cinnamon	2¼ tsp.
1 cup	butter, softened	½ cup
1½ cups	granulated sugar	¾ cup
4	eggs	2
2 tsp.	vanilla	1 tsp.
1 16-oz. pkg.	frozen unsweetened pitted tart red cherries, thawed and drained	½ 16-oz. pkg.

1. Preheat oven to 350°F. Coat a 13×9×2-inch baking pan with nonstick cooking spray; set aside. In a small bowl stir together sour cream and baking soda; set aside. In a medium bowl stir together flour and baking powder; set aside. For topping, in a small bowl stir together brown sugar, walnuts, and cinnamon; set aside.

2. In a large mixing bowl beat butter with an electric mixer on medium to high for 30 seconds. Gradually add granulated sugar, ¼ cup at a time, beating on medium after each addition until well combined (about 3 minutes). Scrape side of bowl; continue beating on medium for 2 minutes more. Add eggs, one at a time, beating well after each addition. Beat in vanilla. Alternately add flour mixture and sour cream mixture, beating on low after each addition just until combined. Beat on medium to high for 20 seconds more.

3. Spread half of the batter in the prepared pan. Top evenly with cherries. Sprinkle one-third of the topping over the cherries. Spread the remaining batter over topping. Sprinkle remaining topping over batter.

4. Bake for 60 to 75 minutes or until a wooden toothpick inserted near the center comes out clean. Cool in pan on a wire rack for 30 minutes; serve warm.

FOR 8 SERVINGS: Prepare using method above, except in Step 1 use an 8×8×2-inch baking pan.

PER SERVING 460 *cal., 22 g total fat (12 g sat. fat), 96 mg chol., 322 mg sodium, 62 g carbo., 2 g fiber, 7 g pro.*

Pineapple-Cream Cheese Cake

Few sweets are as pretty and delicious as a marbled cake. The marbling technique is simple. A few figure eights with a table knife create the lovely look.

1. Preheat oven to 350°F. Grease and lightly flour a 13×9×2-inch baking pan; set aside.

2. In a large mixing bowl stir together flour, 2 cups sugar, baking powder, baking soda, and salt. In a medium bowl combine 2 eggs, pineapple, and 1 teaspoon vanilla. Add pineapple mixture to flour mixture, beating with an electric mixer on low just until combined. Pour batter into the prepared baking pan, spreading evenly.

3. Wash beaters. In a medium bowl beat cream cheese on medium until fluffy. Beat in 1 egg, ¼ cup sugar, and 1 teaspoon vanilla until combined. Drop spoonfuls of cream cheese mixture over batter in pan. Using a table knife, swirl mixtures to marble. Sprinkle with Coconut Topping.

4. Bake about 45 minutes or until a wooden toothpick inserted in the center comes out clean. Cool in pan on a wire rack for 30 minutes. Serve warm.

COCONUT TOPPING: In a small bowl combine ¾ cup packed brown sugar, ¾ cup broken pecans, and ¾ cup flaked or shredded coconut.

FOR 6 SERVINGS: Prepare using method above, except in Step 1 use an 8×8×2-inch baking pan. In Step 2 use 1 cup sugar, 1 egg, and ½ teaspoon vanilla. In Step 3 use the egg yolk, 2 tablespoons sugar, and ½ teaspoon vanilla.

PER SERVING 489 cal., 15 g total fat (7 g sat. fat), 74 mg chol., 249 mg sodium, 84 g carbo., 2 g fiber, 7 g pro.

PREP: 25 minutes   BAKE: 45 minutes
COOL: 30 minutes
OVEN: 350°F

12 servings	ingredients	6 servings
2½ cups	all-purpose flour	1¼ cups
2 cups	sugar	1 cup
1½ tsp.	baking powder	¾ tsp.
½ tsp.	baking soda	¼ tsp.
¼ tsp.	salt	⅛ tsp.
2	eggs, lightly beaten	1
1 20-oz. can	crushed pineapple (juice pack), undrained	1 8-oz. can
1 tsp.	vanilla	½ tsp.
1 8-oz. pkg.	cream cheese, softened	½ 8-oz. pkg.
1	egg	1 egg yolk
¼ cup	sugar	2 Tbsp.
1 tsp.	vanilla	½ tsp.
1 recipe	Coconut Topping	½ recipe

Blueberry Sugar Shortcake with Warm Peach Compote

This is a classic biscuitlike shortcake, the kind that welcomes juicy caramelized peaches into the depths of its rich and tender crumb. Once you taste it, you'll never resort to store-bought sponge cakes again.

1. Preheat oven to 375°F. Grease a large baking sheet; set aside. In a large bowl stir together flour, baking powder, salt, and the ⅔ cup granulated sugar; gently stir in blueberries. Add cream, stirring with a fork just until moistened.

2. Turn out onto prepared baking sheet. Pat dough into two 6-inch circles; cut each into 8 wedges. Separate wedges slightly. Brush tops and sides with melted butter; sprinkle tops with the ¼ cup granulated sugar. Bake for 35 to 40 minutes or until golden and a toothpick inserted in center comes out clean. Cool on baking sheet for 5 minutes. Transfer to a wire rack; cool completely.

3. For peach compote, peel peaches and slice. In a large nonstick skillet melt the 6 tablespoons butter over medium-high heat. Stir in brown sugar; cook about 2 minutes or until brown sugar starts to melt. Add peaches; cook for 3 to 4 minutes or until peaches are heated through, stirring occasionally.

4. Beat 1 cup whipping cream until soft peaks form (tips curl). To assemble, split each shortcake in half. Place bottom of shortcake on a serving plate. Spoon peach compote onto bottom half and top with whipped cream. Replace top half of shortcake. If desired, serve with additional whipped cream. If desired, sprinkle with fresh blueberries.

FOR 8 SERVINGS: Prepare using method above, except in Step 1 use the ⅓ cup granulated sugar. In Step 2 pat dough into one 6-inch circle; sprinkle top with 2 tablespoons granulated sugar. In Step 3 use 3 tablespoons butter. In Step 4 beat ½ cup whipping cream.

PER SERVING 410 cal., 19 g total fat (12 g sat. fat), 60 mg chol., 410 mg sodium, 58 g carbo., 2 g fiber, 4 g pro.

PREP: 35 minutes
BAKE: 35 minutes
COOL: 5 minutes
OVEN: 375°F

16 servings	ingredients	8 servings
4½ cups	all-purpose flour	2¼ cups
2 Tbsp.	baking powder	1 Tbsp.
2 tsp.	salt	1 tsp.
⅔ cup	granulated sugar	⅓ cup
2 cups	fresh blueberries	1 cup
2⅔ cups	whipping cream	1⅓ cups
4 Tbsp.	unsalted butter, melted	2 Tbsp.
¼ cup	granulated sugar	2 Tbsp.
16	ripe peaches	8
6 Tbsp.	butter	3 Tbsp.
⅔ cup	packed brown sugar	⅓ cup
1 cup	whipping cream	½ cup
	Whipped cream (optional)	
	Fresh blueberries (optional)	

Crimson Cranberry-Apple Crisp

Homespun desserts like this one make busy holiday meals extra special. Choose from baking apples such as Rome, McIntosh, or Granny Smith—or combine apple varieties to make your comforting crisp your very own.

1. Preheat oven to 375°F. In a small bowl combine granulated sugar and cinnamon. Place the apples and cranberries in an ungreased 3-quart casserole. Sprinkle sugar-cinnamon mixture over fruit. Toss gently to coat. Bake, covered, for 25 minutes.

2. For topping, in a small bowl combine oats, brown sugar, flour, and nutmeg. With a pastry blender, cut in butter until mixture resembles coarse crumbs. If desired, stir in coconut. Sprinkle topping over partially cooked fruit mixture.

3. Return to oven and bake for 15 to 20 minutes more or until fruit is tender and topping is golden. Transfer to cooling rack; cool slightly. Serve warm. If desired, serve with ice cream.

FOR 6 SERVINGS: Prepare using method above, except in Step 1 use a 1½-quart casserole.

PER SERVING *205 cal., 7 g total fat (4 g sat. fat), 16 mg chol., 66 mg sodium, 36 g carbo., 4 g fiber, 2 g pro.*

PREP: 25 minutes
BAKE: 40 minutes
OVEN: 375°F

12 servings	ingredients	6 servings
½ to ⅔ cup	granulated sugar	¼ to ⅓ cup
2 tsp.	ground cinnamon	1 tsp.
6 cups	sliced, peeled cooking apples	3 cups
4 cups	cranberries	2 cups
1 cup	quick-cooking or regular rolled oats	½ cup
½ cup	packed brown sugar	¼ cup
¼ cup	all-purpose flour	2 Tbsp.
½ tsp.	ground nutmeg or ground ginger	¼ tsp.
6 Tbsp.	butter	3 Tbsp.
¼ cup	chopped coconut or chopped nuts (see note, page 102) (optional)	2 Tbsp.
	Vanilla ice cream, frozen yogurt, or half-and-half (optional)	

Salted Almond Brownies

In professional baking, salt and smoke are today's most fashionable flavors. Both have an uncanny ability to accentuate the flavor of chocolate in a most enticing way, as they do in these bodacious brownies.

1. Preheat oven to 350°F. Line a 13×9×2-inch baking pan with foil, extending foil over the edges of the pan. Grease foil; set pan aside. In a medium saucepan heat and stir unsweetened chocolate and butter over low heat just until melted and smooth.

2. Stir sugar into the melted chocolate mixture. Add eggs, one at a time, beating with a wooden spoon just until combined. Stir in vanilla. In a small bowl stir together flour, cocoa powder, and baking soda. Add flour mixture to chocolate mixture; stir just until combined. Stir in 1½ cups of the milk chocolate pieces. Spread the batter evenly in the prepared pan. Sprinkle remaining chocolate pieces, almonds, and salt over batter.

3. Bake for 25 minutes. Cool in pan on a wire rack. Use foil to lift uncut brownies out of pan. Cut into brownies.

FOR 16 SERVINGS: Prepare using method above, except in Step 1 use a 9×9×2-inch baking pan. In Step 2 stir in ¾ cup of the milk chocolate pieces.

PER SERVING 344 cal., 19 g total fat (11 g sat. fat), 59 mg chol., 140 mg sodium, 42 g carbo., 3 g fiber, 5 g pro.

PREP: **25 minutes**
BAKE: **25 minutes**
OVEN: **350°F**

32 servings	ingredients	16 servings
8 oz.	unsweetened chocolate, chopped	4 oz.
1 cup	butter	½ cup
3 cups	sugar	1½ cups
6	eggs	3
2 tsp.	vanilla	1 tsp.
2 cups	all-purpose flour	1 cup
2 Tbsp.	unsweetened cocoa powder	1 Tbsp.
½ tsp.	baking soda	¼ tsp.
2 cups	milk chocolate pieces	1 cup
3 cups	chopped smoked almonds	1½ cups
½ tsp.	sea salt	¼ tsp.

Macaroon-Chocolate Bars

PREP: 40 minutes
BAKE: 33 minutes
CHILL: 30 minutes
OVEN: 350°F

48 servings	ingredients	24 servings
2 cups	crushed chocolate sandwich cookies with white filling	1 cup
½ cup	sugar	¼ cup
⅓ cup	unsweetened cocoa powder	2 Tbsp.
½ cup	butter, melted	¼ cup
1 tsp.	vanilla	½ tsp.
⅔ cup	all-purpose flour	⅓ cup
⅓ cup	sugar	2 Tbsp.
¼ tsp.	salt	⅛ tsp.
2¾ cups	flaked coconut	1⅓ cups
3	egg whites, lightly beaten	2
½ tsp.	vanilla	¼ tsp.
½ cup	semisweet chocolate pieces	¼ cup
1 tsp.	shortening	½ tsp.
	Whole almonds, toasted (see note, page 102) (optional)	

To crush chocolate sandwich cookies quickly and easily, give handfuls of cookies a whirl in a blender or food processor. Plan on approximately 14 cookies to make 1 cup of crumbs.

1. Preheat oven to 350°F. Line a 13×9×2-inch baking pan with foil, extending the foil over edges of pan. Lightly grease foil; set pan aside.

2. For crust, in a large bowl stir together crushed cookies, ½ cup sugar, and cocoa powder. Stir in melted butter and 1 teaspoon vanilla. Press cookie mixture evenly onto the bottom of the prepared baking pan. Bake for 8 minutes.

3. Meanwhile, in a large bowl stir together flour, ⅓ cup sugar, and salt. Stir in coconut. Stir in egg whites and ½ teaspoon vanilla until combined.

4. Spoon coconut mixture onto crust. Using wet hands, carefully press the coconut mixture to edges of pan. Bake for 25 to 28 minutes more or until top is set and lightly browned. Cool in pan on a wire rack.

5. In a small saucepan cook and stir chocolate and shortening over low heat until melted. Drizzle melted chocolate over uncut bars. Chill about 30 minutes or until chocolate is set. Using the edges of the foil, lift uncut bars out of pan. Cut into 24 bars. Cut each bar in half diagonally to make 48 triangles. If desired, garnish each triangle with a whole almond.

FOR 24 SERVINGS: Prepare using method above, except in Step 1 use an 8×8×2-inch baking pan. In Step 2 use ¼ cup sugar and ½ teaspoon vanilla. In Step 3 use 2 tablespoons sugar and ¼ teaspoon vanilla. In Step 5 cut into 12 bars, then cut each bar to make 24 triangles.

PER SERVING 85 cal., 5 g total fat (3 g sat. fat), 5 mg chol., 51 mg sodium, 10 g carbo., 1 g fiber, 1 g pro.

Peanut Butter-Chocolate Squares

The thin, dark wafer cookies that make the incredible crust may not be available year-round. They're usually stocked during the holidays, so grab a few boxes then and pop them in your freezer.

1. Preheat oven to 325°F. Line a 13×9×2-inch baking pan with foil, extending the foil over edges of pan; set aside. For crust, in a medium bowl stir together crushed cookies, brown sugar, and salt. Stir in melted butter and vanilla. Press cookie mixture evenly onto the bottom of the prepared baking pan. Bake for 8 to 10 minutes or until firm. Cool on a wire rack.

2. In a large bowl whisk together milk, peanut butter, and pudding mixes until combined (mixture will be stiff). Fold in one-fourth of the whipped topping and 1 cup peanuts. Pour peanut butter mixture over crust, spreading evenly. Cover and chill for at least 1 hour.

3. Microwave dipping chocolate according to package directions until melted; transfer to a medium bowl. Fold in the remaining whipped topping. Spread chocolate mixture evenly over peanut butter layer. Cover and chill for 4 to 24 hours.

4. Using the edges of the foil, lift uncut bars out of pan. Cut into bars. If desired, garnish with peanut butter cups and/or additional peanuts.

FOR 12 SERVINGS: Prepare using method above, except in Step 1 use an 8×8×2-inch baking pan. In Step 2 fold in ½ cup peanuts.

PER SERVING 299 cal., 18 g total fat (8 g sat. fat), 12 mg chol., 309 mg sodium, 31 g carbo., 2 g fiber, 6 g pro.

PREP: 30 minutes
BAKE: 8 minutes
CHILL: 5 hours
OVEN: 325°F

24 servings	ingredients	12 servings
2 cups	finely crushed chocolate wafer cookies	1 cup
½ cup	packed brown sugar	¼ cup
¼ tsp.	salt	⅛ tsp.
½ cup	butter, melted	¼ tsp.
1 tsp.	vanilla	½ tsp.
1½ cups	milk	¾ cup
1 cup	peanut butter	½ cup
2 4-serving-size pkg.	French vanilla instant pudding and pie filling mix	1 4-serving-size pkg.
1 8-oz. container	frozen whipped dessert topping, thawed	½ 8-oz. container
1 cup	dry-roasted peanuts, coarsely chopped	½ cup
1 7-oz. tub	dipping chocolate	½ 7-oz. tub
	Miniature chocolate-covered peanut butter cups and/or chopped dry-roasted peanuts (optional)	

Chocolate Carnutty Bars

Cake mix is the secret ingredient in the scrumptious streusel that tops these ridiculously rich caramel-chocolate-peanut bars. Neufchâtel boasts the same flavor and texture of regular cream cheese but contains a third fewer calories.

PREP: 20 minutes
BAKE: 30 minutes
OVEN: 350°F

24 servings	ingredients	12 servings
	Nonstick cooking spray	
1 pkg. 2-layer-size	white cake mix	1 pkg. 1-layer-size*
1 cup	quick-cooking rolled oats	½ cup
½ cup	peanut butter	¼ cup
1	egg, lightly beaten	1 egg yolk
2 Tbsp.	milk	1 Tbsp.
1 8-oz. pkg.	reduced-fat cream cheese (Neufchâtel)	½ 8-oz. pkg.
1 12.25-oz. jar	caramel-flavor ice cream topping	½ 12.25-oz. jar
1 11.5-oz. pkg.	milk chocolate pieces	½ 11.5-oz. pkg.
½ cup	cocktail peanuts	1 cup

1. Preheat oven to 350°F. Coat a 13×9×2-inch baking pan with cooking spray; set aside. For crumb mixture, in a large bowl combine cake mix and oats. Using a pastry blender, cut in peanut butter until mixture resembles fine crumbs. In a small bowl combine egg and milk; stir into crumb mixture. Reserve ¾ cup of the mixture for topping. Press the remaining mixture evenly onto the bottom of the prepared baking pan.

2. For filling, in a medium mixing bowl beat cream cheese with an electric mixer on medium until smooth. Beat in caramel topping. Carefully spread over crumb mixture in pan. Sprinkle with chocolate pieces and peanuts. Top with the reserved crumb mixture.

3. Bake for 30 minutes. Cool in pan on a wire rack. Cut into bars. Store, covered, in the refrigerator.

FOR 12 SERVINGS: Prepare using method above, except in Step 1 use an 8×8×2-inch baking pan. Reserve ⅓ cup of the mixture for topping.

PER SERVING *311 cal., 14 g total fat (5 g sat. fat), 16 mg chol., 273 mg sodium, 41 g carbo., 1 g fiber, 7 g pro.*

*NOTE: If you are unable to find a 1-layer white cake mix, use half the 2-layer white cake mix (about 1¼ cups).

Four-Nut and Maple Bars

Better-for-you whole wheat flour and protein-packed nuts meet pure maple syrup in these dense and chewy bars. For fabulous flavor, use pure maple syrup rather than maple-flavor pancake syrup.

PREP: 20 minutes
BAKE: 25 minutes
OVEN: 350°F

24 servings	ingredients	12 servings
2 cups	whole wheat flour	1 cup
1 tsp.	baking powder	½ tsp.
1 tsp.	baking soda	½ tsp.
2	egg whites	1
¾ cup	pure maple syrup	⅓ cup
½ cup	canola oil	¼ cup
½ cup	fat-free milk	¼ cup
½ cup	chopped cashews	¼ cup
½ cup	slivered almonds, toasted*	¼ cup
½ cup	chopped walnuts, toasted*	¼ cup
1 cup	semisweet chocolate pieces	½ cup
1 recipe	Chocolate-Hazelnut Frosting	½ recipe
⅔ cup	pecan halves, chopped cashews, slivered almonds, and/or chopped walnuts, toasted* (see note, page 102)	⅓ cup

1. Preheat oven to 350°F. Grease and lightly flour a 13×9×2-inch baking pan; set aside.

2. In large bowl combine flour, baking powder, and baking soda. In another bowl whisk together egg whites, maple syrup, oil, and milk; add to flour mixture. Stir to combine. Stir in ½ cup each cashews, almonds, walnuts, and the 1 cup chocolate pieces. Spread in prepared pan.

3. Bake 25 to 30 minutes or until a toothpick inserted near center comes out clean. Cool on wire rack. Spread with Chocolate-Hazelnut Frosting; sprinkle with pecans, cashews, almonds, and/or walnuts. Cut into bars.

CHOCOLATE-HAZELNUT FROSTING: In a bowl combine ¼ cup chocolate-hazelnut spread, 3 tablespoons fat-free milk, and 1 tablespoon pure maple syrup. Stir in ½ cup unsweetened cocoa powder. Gradually stir in 1 to 1¼ cups powdered sugar to reach spreading consistency. Makes ¾ cup.

FOR 12 SERVINGS: Prepare using method above, except in Step 1 use an 8×8×2-inch baking pan. In Step 2 stir in ¼ cup each cashews, almonds, and walnuts, and ½ cup chocolate pieces.

PER SERVING *241 cal., 14 g total fat (2 g sat. fat), 0 mg chol., 81 mg sodium, 29 g carbo., 3 g fiber, 4 g pro.*

Dark Chocolate Chewies

There's nothing like a no-bake cookie for a swift chocolate fix. If you find yourself with old-fashioned rolled oats rather than quick-cooking oats, just give the oats a quick whiz in a blender to break them into smaller flakes.

1. Line an extra-large baking sheet with waxed paper; set aside. In a large saucepan bring sugar, butter, and half-and-half to boiling, stirring to dissolve sugar. Remove from heat. Stir in chocolate pieces, cocoa, vanilla, and mint extract. Stir until chocolate melts and mixture is smooth. Stir in oats, coconut, and almonds.

2. Drop by rounded teaspoons onto prepared baking sheet or into paper bake cups set on baking sheet. Let stand about 1 hour or until set.

PER SERVING *113 cal., 5 g total fat (3 g sat. fat), 7 mg chol., 25 mg sodium, 16 g carbo., 1 g fiber, 1 g pro.*

PREP: 20 minutes
STAND: 1 hour

42 servings	ingredients	21 servings
2 cups	sugar	1 cup
½ cup	butter	¼ cup
½ cup	half-and-half or light cream	¼ cup
¾ cup	dark chocolate pieces	⅓ cup
¼ cup	unsweetened cocoa powder	2 Tbsp.
1 tsp.	vanilla	½ tsp.
¼ tsp.	mint extract	⅛ tsp.
2 cups	quick-cooking rolled oats	1 cup
1 cup	sweetened flaked coconut	½ cup
½ cup	toasted sliced or coarsely chopped almonds (see note, page 102)	¼ cup

Caramel-Cashew Bars

A quintet of buttery-rich ingredients—crushed shortbread, butter, caramels, whipping cream, and cashews—put these sweeties in the winner's circle.

PREP: 15 minutes
BAKE: 23 minutes
OVEN: 325°F

24 servings	ingredients	12 servings
3 cups (1½ 10-oz. pkg.)	finely crushed shortbread cookies	1½ cups (¾ 10-oz. pkg.)
½ cup	butter, melted	¼ cup
¼ cup	sugar	2 Tbsp.
36	vanilla caramels, unwrapped	18
½ cup	whipping cream	¼ cup
2 cups	coarsely chopped cashews or dry-roasted peanuts	1 cup
2 cups	tiny marshmallows	1 cup

1. Preheat oven to 325°F. Line a 13×9×2-inch baking pan with foil, extending foil over the edges of the pan. Lightly grease foil; set pan aside.

2. In a large bowl stir together crushed shortbread cookies, butter, and sugar. Press cookie mixture firmly and evenly over bottom of prepared pan. Bake about 15 minutes or until crust is golden and dried around edges. Cool in pan on a wire rack.

3. Meanwhile, in a heavy medium-size saucepan heat and stir caramels and cream over medium-low heat until melted and smooth. Stir in nuts. Sprinkle marshmallows evenly over baked shortbread crust. Pour caramel mixture over marshmallows; carefully spread evenly.

4. Bake for 8 to 10 minutes or until caramel is set and bubbly around edges. Cool in pan on a wire rack. Use foil to lift uncut bars out of pan. Place on cutting board; cut into bars.

FOR 12 SERVINGS: Prepare using method above, except in Step 1 use an 8×8×2-inch baking pan.

PER SERVING *317 cal., 18 g total fat (8 g sat. fat), 22 mg chol., 245 mg sodium, 34 g carbo., 1 g fiber, 4 g pro.*

Apple-Cinnamon Streusel Bars

No apple peeling is required to make these rich and creamy apple bars. Ready-to-use dried apples do the trick, bringing concentrated apple flavor to this quick and easy fall dessert.

1. Preheat oven to 350°F. For crust, in a large bowl stir together flour, oats, granulated sugar, the 2 teaspoons cinnamon, and ginger. Using a pastry blender, cut in butter until mixture resembles coarse crumbs. For topping, set aside 1 cup of the crust mixture. Press remaining crust mixture evenly and firmly onto the bottom of a 13×9×2-inch baking pan; set aside.

2. For filling, in a medium bowl beat cream cheese, apples, walnuts, sweetened condensed milk, maple syrup, and the 1 teaspoon cinnamon with an electric mixer on medium until well combined. Spread filling over crust in pan. Sprinkle evenly with reserved topping.

3. Bake for 35 to 40 minutes or until topping is light brown. Cool in pan on a wire rack.

4. For icing, in a small bowl stir together powdered sugar and enough of the milk to make icing drizzling consistency. Drizzle over uncut bars. To serve, cut into bars.

FOR 16 SERVINGS: Prepare using method above, except in Step 1 use an 8×8×2-inch baking pan, use the 1 teaspoon cinnamon, and set aside ½ cup of the crust mixture. In Step 2 use ½ teaspoon cinnamon.

PER SERVING *203 cal., 10 g total fat (6 g sat. fat), 25 mg chol., 72 mg sodium, 25 g carbo., 1 g fiber, 3 g pro.*

PREP: 30 minutes
BAKE: 35 minutes
OVEN: 350°F

32 servings	ingredients	16 servings
2 cups	all-purpose flour	1 cup
1½ cups	rolled oats	¾ cup
¾ cup	granulated sugar	⅓ cup
2 tsp.	ground cinnamon	1 tsp.
1 tsp.	ground ginger	½ tsp.
1 cup	butter, cut into pieces	½ cup
1 8-oz. pkg.	cream cheese, softened	½ 8-oz. pkg.
½ cup	finely chopped dried apples	¼ cup
½ cup	chopped walnuts, toasted	¼ cup
½ cup	sweetened condensed milk	¼ cup
¼ cup	pure maple syrup	2 Tbsp.
1 tsp.	ground cinnamon	½ tsp.
1 cup	powdered sugar	½ cup
3 to 4 tsp.	milk	1½ to 2 tsp.

Toasty-Roasty Cheer Bars

The famous doughnut-shape oat cereal makes these crunchy bars a lunch box favorite. Another time try butterscotch- or peanut butter-flavor baking chips for variety.

PREP: 30 minutes
STAND: 30 minutes

32 servings	ingredients	16 servings
1 10.5-oz. pkg.	tiny marshmallows	½ 10.5-oz. pkg.
¼ cup	butter, cut up	2 Tbsp.
2 tsp.	vanilla	1 tsp.
8 cups	round toasted oat cereal with nuts and honey	4 cups
1 cup	lightly salted cashews, coarsely chopped	½ cup
½ cup	coarsely crushed peanut brittle or toffee pieces	¼ cup
1 cup	chocolate-covered peanuts, whole or coarsely chopped	½ cup
1 cup	caramel baking bits	½ cup
1 Tbsp.	water	1½ tsp.
3 oz.	semisweet or bittersweet chocolate, chopped	1½ oz.
¼ tsp.	shortening	⅛ tsp.

1. In a large microwave-safe bowl combine marshmallows and butter. Heat on high for 1½ to 2 minutes or until mixture is puffed and melted, stirring once. Add vanilla; stir until mixture is smooth. Gently stir in cereal, cashews, and peanut brittle. Carefully stir in chocolate-covered peanuts. Press mixture onto the bottom of a greased 13×9×2-inch baking pan.

2. In a small microwave-safe bowl combine caramel bits and the water. Heat on high for 1 to 1½ minutes or until melted, stirring once. Drizzle evenly over bars.

3. In another small microwave-safe bowl combine chocolate and shortening. Heat on high for 1 to 1½ minutes or until melted and smooth, stirring every 30 seconds. Drizzle over bars. Let stand about 30 minutes or until set. Cut into bars.

FOR 16 SERVINGS: Prepare using method above, except in Step 1 use an 8×8×2-inch baking pan.

PER SERVING *172 cal., 7 g total fat (3 g sat. fat), 5 mg chol., 107 mg sodium, 25 g carbo., 1 g fiber, 2 g pro.*

Homemade Oatmeal Cream Pies

Fans of these old-fashioned packaged treats will flip when they taste the homemade version fresh from your oven. Lining the cookie sheet with parchment paper makes cleanup a snap.

1. Preheat oven to 350°F. Grease a cookie sheet; set aside. In a bowl combine flour, baking soda, salt, and baking powder; set aside. In a mixing bowl beat butter and peanut butter with an electric mixer on medium to high until combined. Beat in granulated sugar and brown sugar until fluffy. Beat in egg and vanilla just until combined. Stir in flour mixture and oats just until combined. Drop dough by rounded teaspoons 2 inches apart onto prepared cookie sheet.

2. Bake for 8 to 10 minutes or until edges are light brown and centers are set. Cool on cookie sheet for 1 minute. Transfer cookies to a wire rack and let cool.

3. Meanwhile, for filling, in a mixing bowl combine the hot water and salt. Stir until salt dissolves. Add marshmallow creme, shortening, and powdered sugar. Beat with an electric mixer on medium until combined.

4. Spread 1 tablespoon marshmallow filling onto the flat sides of half the cookies. (Or use an offset spatula to spread marshmallow filling on cookies.) Top filling with another cookie, flat side down.

PER SERVING *367 cal., 20 g total fat (8 g sat. fat), 35 mg chol., 305 mg sodium, 43 g carbo., 1 g fiber, 5 g pro.*

PREP: 40 minutes
BAKE: 8 minutes per batch
OVEN: 350°F

26 servings	ingredients	13 servings
1½ cup	all-purpose flour	¾ cup
1 tsp.	baking soda	½ tsp.
1 tsp.	salt	½ tsp.
½ tsp.	baking powder	¼ tsp.
1 cup	butter, softened	½ cup
1 cup	peanut butter	½ cup
1 cup	granulated sugar	½ cup
1 cup	packed brown sugar	½ cup
2	eggs	1
2 tsp.	vanilla	1 tsp.
2 cups	quick-cooking oats	1 cup
4 tsp.	hot water	2 tsp.
½ tsp.	salt	¼ tsp.
2 7-oz. jars	marshmallow creme	1 7-oz. jar
1 cup	shortening	½ cup
⅔ cup	powdered sugar	⅓ cup

Index

Metric Information

PRODUCT DIFFERENCES

Most of the ingredients called for in the recipes in this book are available in most countries. However, some are known by different names. Here are some common American ingredients and their possible counterparts:

- Sugar (white) is granulated, fine granulated, or castor sugar.
- Powdered sugar is icing sugar.
- All-purpose flour is enriched, bleached, or unbleached white household flour. When self-rising flour is used in place of all-purpose flour in a recipe that calls for leavening, omit the leavening agent (baking soda or baking powder) and salt.
- Light-color corn syrup is golden syrup.
- Cornstarch is cornflour.
- Baking soda is bicarbonate of soda.
- Vanilla or vanilla extract is vanilla essence.
- Green, red, or yellow sweet peppers are capsicums or bell peppers.
- Golden raisins are sultanas.

VOLUME AND WEIGHT

The United States traditionally uses cup measures for liquid and solid ingredients. The chart (above right) shows the approximate imperial and metric equivalents. If you are accustomed to weighing solid ingredients, the following approximate equivalents will be helpful.

- 1 cup butter, castor sugar, or rice = 8 ounces = ½ pound = 250 grams
- 1 cup flour = 4 ounces = ¼ pound = 125 grams
- 1 cup icing sugar = 5 ounces = 150 grams
- Canadian and U.S. volume for a cup measure is 8 fluid ounces (237 ml), but the standard metric equivalent is 250 ml.
- 1 British imperial cup is 10 fluid ounces.
- In Australia, 1 tablespoon equals 20 ml, and there are 4 teaspoons in the Australian tablespoon.
- Spoon measures are used for small amounts of ingredients. Although the size of the tablespoon varies slightly in different countries, for practical purposes and for recipes in this book, a straight substitution is all that's necessary. Measurements made using cups or spoons always should be level unless stated otherwise.

COMMON WEIGHT RANGE REPLACEMENTS

Imperial / U.S.	Metric
½ ounce	15 g
1 ounce	25 g or 30 g
4 ounces (¼ pound)	115 g or 125 g
8 ounces (½ pound)	225 g or 250 g
16 ounces (1 pound)	450 g or 500 g
1¼ pounds	625 g
1½ pounds	750 g
2 pounds or 2¼ pounds	1,000 g or 1 Kg

OVEN TEMPERATURE EQUIVALENTS

Fahrenheit Setting	Celsius Setting	Gas Setting
300°F	150°C	Gas Mark 2 (very low)
325°F	160°C	Gas Mark 3 (low)
350°F	180°C	Gas Mark 4 (moderate)
375°F	190°C	Gas Mark 5 (moderate)
400°F	200°C	Gas Mark 6 (hot)
425°F	220°C	Gas Mark 7 (hot)
450°F	230°C	Gas Mark 8 (very hot)
475°F	240°C	Gas Mark 9 (very hot)
500°F	260°C	Gas Mark 10 (extremely hot)
Broil	Broil	Grill

*Electric and gas ovens may be calibrated using celsius. However, for an electric oven, increase celsius setting 10 to 20 degrees when cooking above 160°C. For convection or forced air ovens (gas or electric), lower the temperature setting 25°F/10°C when cooking at all heat levels.

BAKING PAN SIZES

Imperial / U.S.	Metric
9×1½-inch round cake pan	22- or 23×4-cm (1.5 L)
9×1½-inch pie plate	22- or 23×4-cm (1 L)
8×8×2-inch square cake pan	20×5-cm (2 L)
9×9×2-inch square cake pan	22- or 23×4.5-cm (2.5 L)
11×7×1½-inch baking pan	28×17×4-cm (2 L)
2-quart rectangular baking pan	30×19×4.5-cm (3 L)
13×9×2-inch baking pan	34×22×4.5-cm (3.5 L)
15×10×1-inch jelly roll pan	40×25×2-cm
9×5×3-inch loaf pan	23×13×8-cm (2 L)
2-quart casserole	2 L

U.S./STANDARD METRIC EQUIVALENTS

⅛ teaspoon = 0.5 ml	
¼ teaspoon = 1 ml	
½ teaspoon = 2 ml	
1 teaspoon = 5 ml	
1 tablespoon = 15 ml	
2 tablespoons = 25 ml	
¼ cup = 2 fluid ounces = 50 ml	
⅓ cup = 3 fluid ounces = 75 ml	
½ cup = 4 fluid ounces = 125 ml	
⅔ cup = 5 fluid ounces = 150 ml	
¾ cup = 6 fluid ounces = 175 ml	
1 cup = 8 fluid ounces = 250 ml	
2 cups = 1 pint = 500 ml	
1 quart = 1 litre	